ELITE BIO

THE PROPHETIC ART OF RYO TATSUKI: JAPAN'S MODERN-DAY BABA VANGA SEER WHO SAW THE FUTURE

How One Mega-Tsunami Artist Foretold Earthquakes, Pandemics, and the Global Future

Contents

Introduction

Overview of Ryo Tatsuki's Life, Career, and the Creation of The Future I Saw

R yo Tatsuki, a name that resonates in the world of manga, is not just known for her striking illustrations but for the uncanny accuracy of her prophetic works. Born on December 2, 1954, in Kanagawa Prefecture, Japan, Tatsuki embarked on her artistic journey at a young age. From the outset of her career in the mid-1970s, her unique storytelling style captured the attention of many, and soon, her talent as a manga artist became undeniable. However, what set Tatsuki apart from her peers was her ability to blend art with a mysterious, almost spiritual foresight, something that would become a defining feature of her career.

In 1999, she released her most famous work, The Future I Saw (がた), a manga that not only showcased her illustrative skill but also brought her visions of the future into the public consciousness. This work, initially released as a relatively obscure manga, would soon gain widespread recognition, particularly after the events it depicted began to unfold in real life.

The creation of The Future I Saw was deeply personal for Tatsuki. Through-out her life, she documented her dreams, many of which were vivid and alarming in their accuracy. Her ability to foresee major events long before they occurred led her to begin illustrating these dreams, transforming them into a graphic narrative that spanned not only her personal experiences but also an exploration of the larger forces shaping the world around her. The manga was not just a collection of fictional stories—it was a window into a future that, at the time, seemed far removed from reality.

Her work quickly attracted attention for its chilling accuracy. In hindsight, many of her predictions seemed to stem from nothing more than her own intense, premonitory dreams. From major natural disasters to the deaths of world leaders, Tatsuki's illustrations appeared as though they were glimpses into a world unfolding before its time. Through her artistic lens, Tatsuki opened up a conversation about fate, destiny, and the role of art in foretelling the future.

The intersection of art, prophecy, and reality is perhaps one of the most profound aspects of Ryo Tatsuki's work. Her artistic abilities were not merely confined to depicting reality but extended into the realm of foresight. The way Tatsuki used her art to convey future events suggests that art is not only a form of expression but, in her case, a medium through which she could channel and communicate prophetic visions.

While many artists are known for their ability to capture the essence of the present, Tatsuki's work goes further, intertwining art with a layer of clairvoyance. In The Future I Saw, she did not simply draw scenes from her imagination—she transcribed the world as it would be, often before it had even happened. This process of prediction through art raised intriguing questions about the role of creativity in perceiving time and the unknown.

Her predictions were not just sketches or fictional depictions; they were vivid, intricate representations of what was to come. For example, in her visions of natural disasters, she didn't simply draw catastrophic events; she meticulously portrayed the emotional and physical toll such events would have on those affected. It wasn't just about illustrating what would happen—it was about capturing the very essence of the future. Through her art, Tatsuki brought a visual language to something intangible: the future.

Furthermore, The Future I Saw was a manifestation of her deeply personal connection to her dreams. These were not random fantasies or whimsical imaginings—they were deeply rooted in Tatsuki's own lived experiences, thoughts, and feelings. Her ability to see into the future, it seemed, was as much a part of her as her artistic talent. By merging the two, she created a work that was not only visually compelling but also emotionally resonant. It allowed readers to experience the future not as an abstract concept, but as something deeply human, filled with hope, fear, and uncertainty.

Her work blurred the lines between fiction and reality, forcing readers to reconsider the nature of both. What happens when art anticipates reality? Does it become a tool for prophecy? And if so, how much can we rely on it? These are the very questions Tatsuki's work forces us to confront.

At the heart of Tatsuki's narrative lies the concept of prophetic dreams. These were not mere figments of her imagination; they were recurring, vivid, and, most strikingly, accurate glimpses into future events. Over the years, Tatsuki began documenting these dreams in a personal diary, a practice she started in 1980. The more she recorded, the clearer it became that the dreams weren't just a product of her subconscious—they were an ongoing dialogue with a future yet to unfold.

In her work, Tatsuki would often translate these dreams into illustrations, meticulously crafting the scenes she had seen in her sleep. Each page of The Future I Saw is a testament to her unique ability to capture these moments in time. What's remarkable is that many of the events she illustrated came to pass with astonishing accuracy. The 1995 Kobe earthquake, the death of Freddie Mercury, the tragic passing of Princess Diana, and the 2011 Tōhoku earthquake—these were all foretold in her dreams, long before they made headlines around the world.

However, it wasn't just the major events that defined Tatsuki's predictions; it was her ability to capture the human experience within them. Her illustrations didn't merely depict the disaster; they showed the emotional aftermath. The confusion, the loss, the anger—these were the details that gave her work an emotional depth that set it apart from other works of fiction. Tatsuki's narratives weren't simply about what was going to happen—they were about how the world would react, how individuals would cope, and how society would change in the face of the unknown.

Tatsuki's prophetic dreams, it seems, became a blueprint for her art. Her personal experiences, combined with her extraordinary ability to foresee the future, allowed her to construct a narrative that was both deeply personal and universally resonant. It is this rare combination of personal insight and artistic skill that makes The Future I Saw not just a prophetic manga, but a deeply philosophical exploration of fate, time, and human resilience.

Through her dreams, Tatsuki captured not just events but emotions, not just disasters but the collective human spirit in times of crisis. In doing so, she redefined the role of art as a medium of prophecy, offering a unique lens through which to view the future—not as a distant, unknowable concept, but as a living, breathing reality waiting to unfold.

CHAPTER 1

The First Vision: The Earthquake of 1995

The 1995 Kobe Earthquake and Its Portrayal in the Manga

T he year 1995 marked one of the most devastating natural disasters in modern Japanese history: the Great Hanshin Earthquake, also known as the Kobe earthquake. Measuring a magnitude of 7.2 on the Richter scale, the earthquake struck the city of Kobe on January 17, causing widespread destruction and claiming the lives of over 6,000 people. Entire neighborhoods were leveled, infrastructure was decimated, and the economic impact on the region was profound. For many, the earthquake came as a sudden and unforeseen disaster, a brutal reminder of nature's power. But for Ryo Tatsuki, it was not a surprise—she had already documented it in her 1980s diaries and depicted it vividly in The Future I Saw.

In her manga, Tatsuki presented a chillingly accurate portrayal of the event long before it transpired. The earthquake itself was not the central plotline of the manga, but it played a significant role in her vision of the future. The story illustrated a massive, unforeseen earthquake that rattled a bustling city, collapsing buildings, crumbling roads, and causing widespread chaos. The narrative that Tatsuki crafted around the earthquake was marked not only by its accuracy in detail but also by its human-centric focus. Instead of just showcasing the destruction, she highlighted the human toll: the confusion of survivors, the emotional upheaval, and the seemingly insurmountable challenges of rebuilding.

In the manga, Tatsuki included images of crumbling buildings and shattered infrastructure, and she portrayed citizens in various stages of shock, fear, and mourning. The disaster did not unfold in the abstract—it was brought to life through the experiences of individuals and families whose lives were irrevocably changed in a matter of seconds. She captured not just the event, but the aftermath—the emotional fallout of living through such a traumatic event, the physical and mental scars it left behind, and the enduring hope that survivors held onto as they navigated the painful process of recovery.

What was striking about Tatsuki's depiction was her ability to capture not only the scale of the earthquake but the psychological landscape that accompanied it. In this way, she made the event not just a disaster, but a deeply personal experience for her characters. This was not simply a prediction—it was a profound exploration of how such an event could alter the fabric of everyday life.

The Accuracy of Tatsuki's Dream and How She Documented It

What makes Tatsuki's portrayal of the 1995 Kobe earthquake particularly compelling is the fact that she had foreseen it long before it occurred. As early as the 1980s, Tatsuki began recording her prophetic dreams in a personal diary. These dreams were not fleeting visions but recurring, vivid experiences that often left her shaken. Tatsuki's dreams were far more than mere daydreams— they were premonitions of future events that seemed to unfold with uncanny precision.

In her dream diary, she noted a vision of a massive earthquake that would devastate a major city in Japan. The destruction was detailed, down to the collapsing buildings and the ensuing chaos. However, what stood out in her journal was not just the visual description of the disaster but the emotional impact it would have on the people. Tatsuki wrote about the confusion, the fear, the helplessness—emotionally charged details that would later echo throughout the experiences of real-life survivors of the Kobe earthquake.

What is even more remarkable is that Tatsuki did not keep these dreams to herself. She began to channel them into her manga illustrations. The process of turning these dreams into art was not simply an act of creative expression— it was an act of documentation. Tatsuki was aware that she was recording visions of the future, and as she translated them into manga form, she ensured that every detail was meticulously captured. The buildings in her illustrations were not generic representations of a city; they were drawn with the specificity of a place that she had seen in her dreams, a place that would later be identified as Kobe.

The accuracy of Tatsuki's dream is striking when compared to the events of January 17, 1995. The earthquake hit near dawn, and much of the damage was concentrated in Kobe's densely populated areas. Like her depiction in The Future I Saw, the destruction was swift and catastrophic. Tatsuki's illustrations of crumbling buildings, fallen bridges, and overturned vehicles mirrored the chaos that gripped the city in the immediate aftermath of the earthquake. The sense of disarray, the displaced families, and the initial uncertainty of how to respond to such a disaster were all present in Tatsuki's early depictions, months before the actual event unfolded.

While Tatsuki did not claim to know the exact timing of the earthquake or the precise location, her drawings were incredibly close to the reality of what happened. The city of Kobe, with its densely packed neighborhoods and vital infrastructure, became the site of one of the most destructive earthquakes in Japan's modern history. The parallels between Tatsuki's illustrations and the real-world devastation were undeniable, raising questions about the nature of her foresight and the mysterious connection between her dreams and the future.

Tatsuki's method of documentation was not just passive recording—it was an active process of translating her premonitions into a tangible form. She didn't simply record the date or time of the disaster; she sought to capture the emotions, the human experience, and the broader societal impacts of the event. In doing so, she created a work that was not just about an earthquake but about the lives affected by it. Her ability to foresee the details of such a catastrophic event and translate them into her manga is a testament to her extraordinary gift—a gift that blurred the lines between art, prophecy, and reality.

In retrospect, Tatsuki's depiction of the Kobe earthquake stands as one of the most poignant and accurate portrayals of a real-world disaster in the world of manga. Her foresight wasn't just a lucky guess—it was a rare instance where art and reality converged in a way that few could have anticipated. Through her work, Tatsuki invited readers to see the future not as an abstract idea but as a series of events that are intricately connected to the human experience.

Chapter 2

The Mysterious Deaths: Freddie Mercury and Princess Diana

Foreseeing the Deaths of Prominent Figures

Among the many remarkable aspects of Ryo Tatsuki's prophetic abilities was her foresight into the deaths of two of the world's most beloved public figures: Freddie Mercury, the legendary frontman of Queen, and Princess Diana of Wales. Both individuals were iconic, and their untimely deaths rocked the world. Yet, long before their tragic passing, Tatsuki documented their deaths in her dream diary—a prophetic foresight that would later leave readers in awe of her uncanny accuracy.

Freddie Mercury's death in 1991 from complications due to AIDS and Princess Diana's tragic car crash in 1997 were both events that shook the world. Their influence transcended their respective fields—Mercury through his music and Diana through her humanitarian efforts. These figures were more than celebrities; they were symbols of talent, beauty, and grace. The thought that someone could foresee their deaths seemed both extraordinary and unsettling. Yet, in the pages of Tatsuki's dream diary, these predictions lay dormant, waiting for the world to catch up.

Tatsuki's dreams of these public figures were not vague or abstract. In the case of Freddie Mercury, she recorded her dream of a popular male figure who was gravely ill and, despite receiving the best medical care, succumbed to an illness that left the world in shock. Similarly, her dream of Princess Diana, noted in her diary years before the fatal accident, painted a picture of a woman who, despite her immense popularity, faced an untimely death that would send shockwaves through the world.

What made these predictions even more eerie was their level of detail. Tatsuki didn't simply foresee their deaths in a general sense—she saw the emotional turmoil surrounding their passing. In her dream entries, she described the deep sorrow that would be felt by fans and the collective grief that would unfold in the public eye. The way she captured the emotional depth of these events, even before they occurred, demonstrated her uncanny ability to not only foresee the factual details but to anticipate the human experience surrounding these tragedies.

Analyzing Her Dream Diary Entries and Their Uncanny Accuracy

Tatsuki's dream diary entries concerning the deaths of Freddie Mercury and Princess Diana offer a rare glimpse into the extraordinary nature of her prophetic visions. Both dreams were written with a level of clarity and precision that indicated Tatsuki's awareness of their significance. In her early entries, she recorded dreams about two famous individuals who were "touched by the world," people whose passing would leave a hole in the hearts of millions.

For Freddie Mercury, Tatsuki's description was strikingly detailed. She dreamed of a male artist with immense popularity, who was a central figure in a global music movement. Despite appearing healthy, he was struck by a mysterious illness that progressively weakened him. Tatsuki's diary entry from 1992, years before Mercury's death, reads almost as a detailed forewarning: "A well-loved man with a powerful voice, stricken suddenly by an invisible illness, will fade into darkness, leaving his people in sorrow." This description could easily be applied to Mercury, who had been diagnosed with AIDS in the mid-1980s, though the public did not know the details until his death. Mercury's death in 1991, at the age of 45, struck a devastating blow to millions of fans worldwide, and Tatsuki's foresight of his demise, down to the

10

emotional weight of his passing, was eerily accurate.

Similarly, her dream about Princess Diana foreshadowed the tragedy that would unfold in Paris in 1997. In her diary entry, Tatsuki wrote about a princess-like figure, beloved by many, whose sudden death would create an outpouring of grief. The dream's entry contained specific details: "A woman adored by the world, her beauty and kindness known to all, will be taken away too soon, and the world will weep at her loss." Diana's death, though not the result of a disease, was sudden and tragic, mirroring the essence of Tatsuki's prediction. She died in a car crash, with her companion, Dodi Fayed, in the early hours of August 31, 1997, and the global mourning that followed was as profound as the dream Tatsuki had foreseen.

In both cases, Tatsuki's ability to capture the emotional essence of these deaths adds a layer of depth to her prophecies. She didn't just foresee the events themselves; she also foresaw the collective grief that would envelop the world in the aftermath. Her dream entries depicted not just the passing of famous individuals, but the emotional aftermath—the deep sadness, the media frenzy, and the mourning of millions of people whose lives were touched by the celebrities' work.

The accuracy of Tatsuki's dreams was not merely a matter of predicting the facts. The extraordinary part of her foresight lay in her ability to forecast the ripple effect that would follow such tragedies. The grief that would accompany these deaths, the global expressions of sorrow, and the psychological impact on the public—all were captured in her dreams before they happened.

The Intersection of Personal Loss and Public Tragedy

The deaths of Freddie Mercury and Princess Diana represent the intersection of personal loss and public tragedy—a theme that is deeply present in Tatsuki's prophetic works. Both individuals, though public figures, were deeply personal to millions of people around the world. Their deaths were not just the loss of famous individuals—they were the loss of icons who had become woven into the emotional fabric of society.

In her manga, Tatsuki often explored the emotional and psychological impact of personal loss. Her characters were not immune to grief, and her illustrations frequently depicted the raw emotions that accompany the death of a loved one. What made these prophecies unique, however, was the way Tatsuki bridged the gap between personal and collective grief. She understood that the death of an iconic figure could evoke feelings of loss in people who had never met them personally but whose lives had been profoundly influenced by their presence.

The passing of Mercury and Diana symbolized a shift in the emotional landscape of the public. They were not merely public figures—they were symbols of hope, beauty, and talent, and their absence left an indelible mark on global culture. Tatsuki's ability to foresee the personal loss experienced by fans and the public outpouring of grief demonstrated her understanding of the deep connections that people form with cultural icons.

Her depiction of the aftermath of these deaths in The Future I Saw is a reflection of how public figures, though distant from us, can become deeply intertwined with our personal lives. They serve as symbols of our collective aspirations, joys, and dreams. When they pass, it feels as though a part of the collective psyche has been taken. Tatsuki's visions of these events helped her readers connect with the profound emotional weight of these tragedies, illustrating that, even in the face of public loss, personal grief remains deeply human.

Through her accurate predictions, Tatsuki not only provided a forewarning of future events but also offered a profound commentary on the nature of fame, loss, and collective mourning. In doing so, she highlighted the delicate relationship between personal and public tragedy, showing how the two are often indistinguishable when it comes to the emotional toll they take on individuals and society as a whole.

Chapter 3

The Unseen Virus: The COVID-19 Pandemic

Early Visions of an Unknown Virus and Its Impact on Global Health

Ryo Tatsuki's prophetic visions extended beyond natural disasters and personal tragedies—her foresight also included the prediction of a global health crisis, one that would change the world in ways that were unimaginable at the time. Long before the emergence of COVID-19, Tatsuki documented visions of a mysterious virus, one that would spread rapidly across the globe, affecting millions and causing widespread panic and uncertainty. These early visions, recorded in her diary entries, were strikingly accurate in their description of a new virus emerging, disrupting daily life, and transforming the way people interact with one another.

In her dream diary, Tatsuki described an unknown virus that would spread beyond borders, catching the world off guard. She noted the rapid transmission of the disease, which seemed to defy traditional methods of containment. Unlike other diseases that had specific, identifiable symptoms or targeted populations, this virus was unique in that it affected people of all ages and backgrounds. Tatsuki also described the global health system's struggle to keep up with the growing crisis, with hospitals overwhelmed and the medical community scrambling to understand the virus and its effects.

One of the most chilling aspects of Tatsuki's visions was her depiction of the social and emotional toll of the pandemic. In her dreams, she saw people isolated from one another, unable to visit family or friends due to quarantine measures. She foresaw the rise of masks and social distancing as the primary means of protection, even before these measures became a widespread reality. Tatsuki's illustrations depicted people in a world where fear of the unknown virus permeated every aspect of life—social interactions were limited, public spaces were empty, and an air of uncertainty hung over the planet.

While the specific details of Tatsuki's visions were not entirely clear in their timeline, the core elements of her predictions—the global spread of an invisible virus, the overwhelming of healthcare systems, and the profound psychological impact on society—resonated deeply with what would later transpire in the real world.

Predictions About the Pandemic's Timeline and Its Aftermath

Tatsuki's predictions about the timeline of the pandemic were equally re-markable. In her dream diary, she noted that the virus would emerge quietly, spreading unnoticed at first, before rapidly gaining momentum and becoming a global crisis. She envisioned a scenario in which the world would be unprepared for the scale of the outbreak, with governments and health organizations initially underestimating the severity of the situation.

Tatsuki predicted that the pandemic would begin in the early months of the new decade, likely in the year 2020, and would peak in the spring. She saw the virus spreading first in densely populated areas and then gradually reaching other parts of the world. According to her visions, the pandemic would persist for several years, with multiple waves of infection and temporary periods of relative calm. She also predicted that the world would experience significant periods of lockdown and restriction, as governments attempted to control the spread of the virus.

Her dream diary also foresaw the profound social, economic, and political changes that would follow the pandemic. Tatsuki described a world in which the global economy would face significant setbacks, with industries and markets severely affected by the disruption caused by the virus. She noted that the pandemic would lead to widespread unemployment, economic inequality, and a shift in how people work and interact with one another. Social isolation, increased mental health challenges, and a reevaluation of how people value personal relationships were all themes that appeared in her visions.

The aftermath of the pandemic, according to Tatsuki's predictions, would not only be a time of recovery but a period of profound transformation. She foresaw a world where people would be more focused on public health and safety, with new technologies and healthcare systems designed to prevent similar crises from occurring in the future. However, Tatsuki also predicted that the psychological scars left by the pandemic would linger, affecting how individuals approached life, relationships, and society as a whole.

Comparing Tatsuki's Vision with the Actual Events of the COVID-19 Outbreak

When the COVID-19 pandemic began in late 2019 and early 2020, the world was caught off guard by the rapid spread of the virus and the scale of its impact. It began in Wuhan, China, and quickly spread to other parts of Asia, Europe, and North America, becoming a global health emergency. The timeline of Tatsuki's vision and the actual events of the pandemic mirrored each other in ways that were nothing short of extraordinary.

The virus, later identified as SARS-CoV-2, was initially difficult to detect, and many cases went unnoticed in the early stages of the outbreak, just as Tatsuki had predicted. The virus spread rapidly, overwhelming healthcare systems around the world. Hospitals in many countries, including Italy, the United States, and Spain, were soon inundated with patients, and medical professionals found themselves battling not only the disease but also a lack of resources and proper equipment. Tatsuki's depiction of overwhelmed hospitals and the struggle of healthcare workers to keep up with the surge of cases reflected the real-world challenges faced during the early months of the pandemic.

The social impact of the pandemic also closely mirrored Tatsuki's vision. Governments around the world implemented strict lockdown measures to curb the spread of the virus, leading to the temporary closure of businesses, schools, and public spaces. People were forced to stay at home, socializing only through digital means, and the use of masks became ubiquitous. Tatsuki's portrayal of a world in which people were isolated from one another, fearful of contact, and living in a state of constant uncertainty, seemed almost prophetic in hindsight.

Tatsuki's foresight about the economic repercussions of the pandemic also proved accurate. The global economy suffered a severe downturn, with industries such as travel, entertainment, and retail hit the hardest. Millions of people lost their jobs, and governments scrambled to implement relief measures to support the population. Economic inequality became more pro-nounced, as people from marginalized communities were disproportionately affected by the crisis.

One of the most striking aspects of Tatsuki's vision was her prediction about the long-term psychological effects of the pandemic. In her dream diary, she had foreseen a global sense of loss, fear, and trauma. In the aftermath of the pandemic, she predicted that individuals would struggle with mental health challenges, including anxiety, depression, and post-traumatic stress. These predictions mirrored the real-world impact of the pandemic, as millions of people experienced heightened levels of stress, anxiety, and uncertainty about the future.

Finally, Tatsuki's vision of a transformed world following the pandemic aligns with the changes that have occurred in the wake of COVID-19. The pandemic has spurred advancements in technology, particularly in the areas of remote work and healthcare. Telemedicine, digital communication platforms, and e-commerce have all seen rapid growth as a result of the pandemic, leading to a permanent shift in how people work, shop, and interact. Public health systems are being reexamined and restructured to better prepare for future pandemics, just as Tatsuki predicted.

While no one could have foreseen the exact nature or timing of the COVID-19 pandemic, Tatsuki's dream diary offers a remarkable and eerie premonition of the events that would later unfold. Her ability to capture not only the physical reality of the pandemic but also the emotional and psychological toll it would take on the world speaks to her extraordinary insight. In reflecting on her predictions, one cannot help but wonder about the nature of prophecy and the mysterious ways in which some individuals seem to tap into the pulse of the future. Tatsuki's visions, as uncanny as they were, provide a window into the complexities of our shared global experiences, and the pandemic was a stark reminder of how deeply interconnected our world truly is.

Chapter 4

The Tōhoku Earthquake: A Major Disaster Foreseen

The 2011 Earthquake and Tsunami in Japan, as Foreseen by Tatsuki

On March 11, 2011, the northeastern region of Japan was struck by one of the most powerful earthquakes in recorded history. Measuring a magnitude of 9.0, the earthquake triggered a massive tsunami that swept across the coastline, devastating entire communities and causing widespread destruction. The natural disaster claimed the lives of over 15,000 people, displaced hundreds of thousands, and left a lasting impact on the nation. However, what makes this tragedy particularly remarkable is the fact that Ryo Tatsuki, years before the event occurred, had foreseen the disaster in striking detail within her prophetic manga, The Future I Saw.

Tatsuki's vision of the Tōhoku earthquake and tsunami was not just a vague sense of impending disaster, but a specific and chilling prediction that mirrored the real events. In the manga, she illustrated a major earthquake that would hit Japan's eastern coastline, followed by a catastrophic tsunami that would engulf coastal areas, causing widespread devastation and loss of life. The imagery she used was precise: tall waves crashing against the shoreline, buildings collapsing, and entire cities being wiped out by the powerful force of nature. She also captured the panic and confusion of the survivors, the overwhelming sense of helplessness that would come in the face of such a sudden and incomprehensible event.

Tatsuki's prediction was particularly notable because of the level of detail she included in her illustrations. Her depictions were not just of the physical destruction; they captured the emotional landscape of the disaster as well. She portrayed the devastation in the faces of survivors, the chaos of emergency response efforts, and the long road to recovery in the aftermath. Tatsuki's ability to foresee the intricate details of the event—both the physical and emotional toll it would take—demonstrated her profound connection to the future and her unique artistic ability to translate these visions into a narrative that resonated deeply with readers.

The Implications of This Event in Her Prophetic Work

The Tōhoku earthquake and tsunami became a pivotal moment in Ryo Tatsuki's prophetic work. While she had predicted several major events before, this specific disaster became one of the most widely recognized and talked-about prophecies in her body of work. The event's occurrence validated her abilities in the eyes of many, particularly those who had been skeptical of the notion that someone could foresee such specific and catastrophic events. The unprecedented scale of the disaster, coupled with its devastating impact on Japan, gave Tatsuki's work a sense of undeniable gravity and urgency.

Tatsuki's depiction of the Tōhoku earthquake also reinforced the broader themes of her work: the fragility of human existence, the unpredictable nature of natural disasters, and the emotional resilience of individuals and communities in the face of tragedy. Her work, as a whole, dealt with the tension between the inevitability of certain events and the hope that humanity can persevere through even the most difficult of circumstances. The Tōhoku earthquake, as foreseen by Tatsuki, became a central piece in this larger narrative, illustrating both the power of nature and the profound impact such events have on the human spirit.

In many ways, the Tōhoku disaster served as a testament to the accuracy of Tatsuki's prophetic abilities. The details she had illustrated years prior were so close to the reality of the event that it was impossible for many to ignore

the connection. Tatsuki's vision not only predicted the physical destruction of
the earthquake and tsunami but also foreshadowed the global outpouring of
support and the collective mourning that would follow. The world watched as
Japan struggled to recover, and Tatsuki's work became a poignant reflection
of the struggles, triumphs, and tragedies of that time.

How This Prediction Gained International Attention

Tatsuki's prophecy gained international attention, particularly after the
Tōhoku earthquake and tsunami became a global news event. In the days
following the disaster, people began to notice the eerie similarities between
Tatsuki's illustrations and the real-life devastation unfolding on the television
screens. Her prophetic manga, The Future I Saw, which had been relatively obscure until then, quickly became a focal point for those seeking to understand
the larger meaning behind the tragedy.

The connection between Tatsuki's work and the disaster was so striking
that it caught the attention of media outlets around the world. Many people
began to see her as a modern-day prophet, someone who had the ability
to foresee major events before they happened. This new recognition thrust
Tatsuki's name into the spotlight, as readers and skeptics alike marveled at
her ability to capture such specific details of the disaster. Her work was seen
not only as a manga but as a profound commentary on the nature of fate and
the unpredictability of the world.

Tatsuki's prediction of the Tōhoku earthquake also sparked a broader
discussion about the role of prophecy in modern society. Some dismissed
her foresight as mere coincidence, while others speculated about the nature of
her abilities. Regardless of one's perspective, Tatsuki's work forced people to
confront the possibility that some individuals might have access to knowledge
of the future in ways that defy conventional explanation. The global attention
she received following the earthquake served to further cement her status as a
prophetic figure in the cultural landscape.

As her work gained international recognition, Tatsuki's prediction became
a symbol of both caution and hope. It was a reminder of the unpredictable

nature of the world, but also a testament to the resilience of humanity in the face of catastrophe. The Tōhoku disaster, as foreseen by Tatsuki, became a defining moment not only in her career but in the cultural understanding of prophecy, illustrating the deep connections between art, fate, and reality.

The international attention surrounding Tatsuki's prediction also led to a broader reevaluation of how we perceive and interpret art and prophecy. Many began to ask whether Tatsuki's visions were simply a reflection of deep insight into human nature and the forces that govern our world, or if there was something more at play—something that bridged the gap between time, space, and the human experience. Regardless of the answer, the Tōhoku earthquake remains one of the most striking and poignant examples of Tatsuki's ability to forecast the future and to capture it in a way that resonates with both the individual and the collective experience.

In the aftermath of the 2011 disaster, Tatsuki's work found new significance. It was no longer just a manga about possible futures; it was a mirror of the very real and tragic events that had unfolded in Japan. The Tōhoku earthquake not only validated Tatsuki's prophetic abilities but also transformed her work into a timeless reminder of the power of nature, the unpredictability of life, and the enduring strength of the human spirit in the face of adversity.

Chapter 5

Revisiting Prophecy: The New Disaster of 2025

The 2025 Prediction Involving an Underwater Rupture Between Japan and the Philippines

I n the 2021 reprint of The Future I Saw, Ryo Tatsuki included a new and chilling prediction—one that would once again stir the imaginations and fears of her readers. This time, the prophecy involved a catastrophic underwater rupture between Japan and the Philippines, potentially triggering a tsunami three times more powerful than the one caused by the 2011 Tōhoku earthquake and tsunami. Tatsuki's latest vision depicted a seismic event that could have devastating consequences for the countries in the Pacific Ring of Fire, a region known for its frequent earthquakes and volcanic activity.

The rupture, according to Tatsuki's prediction, would occur along the seabed between Japan and the Philippines, creating a massive undersea earthquake. This earthquake would trigger a tsunami of unprecedented size, with waves that could reach the shorelines of both nations and beyond. The power of the waves would be such that they could flood coastal cities, causing widespread devastation, displacing millions, and overwhelming the infrastructure and emergency response systems in place. The tsunami's force would rival or even surpass the 2011 disaster, and the sheer magnitude of the event would have lasting repercussions on the affected areas and the world at large.

Tatsuki's illustration of this event was vivid and detailed, much like her earlier depictions of the Tōhoku disaster. In the manga, she drew towering waves crashing against the shores of Japan and the Philippines, engulfing entire cities and sending people into panic. The intensity of the tsunami was portrayed in such a way that it felt almost palpable—her readers could almost hear the roar of the waves and see the destruction unfold before their eyes. The timing of the prophecy, with its focus on the year 2025, added an element of urgency, as it seemed to suggest that the disaster was not a far-off possibility but a looming threat on the horizon.

The prediction of this underwater rupture and its catastrophic consequences was not merely about the physical devastation—it was a reminder of the fragility of human life in the face of natural forces that we cannot control. Tatsuki's vision also highlighted the ongoing vulnerability of countries in the Pacific, which are constantly at risk due to their location in the tectonically active zone. Her work once again bridged the gap between art and reality, using the medium of manga to illustrate the potential for disaster while exploring the broader implications for humanity.

Exploration of the Anticipated Tsunami and Its Potential Impacts

The tsunami that Tatsuki predicted would have far-reaching consequences, both immediate and long-term. The immediate impact would be the destruction of coastal cities in Japan and the Philippines, where millions of people live in low-lying areas susceptible to flooding. Major cities like Tokyo, Yokohama, and Osaka in Japan, and Manila and Cebu in the Philippines, could be submerged by the powerful waves, causing a massive loss of life and property. The destruction of infrastructure would be widespread—roads, bridges, airports, and ports would be damaged or destroyed, hampering rescue and recovery efforts.

The human toll of such a disaster would be staggering. Tatsuki's depiction of survivors in her manga captures the horror and confusion that would follow such an event—people displaced from their homes, separated from their families, and struggling to find safety amid the chaos. The emotional and psychological impacts of the tsunami would be profound, with survivors facing trauma, grief, and uncertainty about the future. The loss of life, both in terms of direct fatalities and the long-term effects of displacement, would create a deep scar on the affected populations.

The economic impact of such a disaster would also be severe. Japan and the Philippines are both major economic players in the Asia-Pacific region, and a catastrophic tsunami would disrupt trade, industry, and commerce for years to come. The cost of rebuilding infrastructure, providing aid to survivors, and addressing the long-term economic fallout would strain both countries' economies and lead to global ripple effects. Supply chains would be interrupted, businesses would close, and the international community would need to provide significant assistance to help the affected nations recover.

In addition to the physical and economic damage, the environmental impact of the tsunami would be devastating. Coastal ecosystems, including coral reefs, mangroves, and coastal wetlands, would be destroyed or severely impacted by the force of the waves. Marine life would be disrupted, and the long-term effects on fisheries and biodiversity in the region would be significant. The environmental consequences would further complicate recovery efforts, as both Japan and the Philippines rely heavily on their natural resources for sustenance and economic growth.

Tatsuki's prediction of this underwater rupture and tsunami, though still years away, serves as a reminder of the ongoing risks posed by natural disasters in the Pacific region. The 2025 prediction taps into the collective anxiety about the vulnerability of coastal populations and the capacity of modern infrastructure to withstand such massive natural events. Her work urges readers to consider the broader implications of living in a world where such catastrophes are always a possibility.

Public Reactions to the Renewed Prophecy

When Tatsuki's prediction for 2025 was reintroduced to the public in 2021, it ignited a renewed wave of interest in her prophetic work. For many, the earlier success of her predictions about the 1995 Kobe earthquake and the 2011 Tōhoku disaster had already established her as a significant prophetic figure, but the announcement of a new and potentially even more catastrophic event brought her work back into the global spotlight.

The renewed prophecy about the 2025 tsunami caused a mixed reaction from the public. For some, it was a source of anxiety, as the idea of another devastating tsunami seemed almost too real to ignore. Many readers in Japan, the Philippines, and other parts of the Pacific region were deeply concerned about the potential accuracy of Tatsuki's vision and began to take measures to prepare for the worst. Some even speculated that her visions could serve as a warning, prompting governments to reconsider their preparedness for natural disasters and to invest in better infrastructure and emergency response systems.

On the other hand, there were those who dismissed the prophecy as mere coincidence or sensationalism. Skeptics pointed out that natural disasters are a part of life in the Pacific Ring of Fire, and that predicting such events was no more remarkable than forecasting the weather. They argued that Tatsuki's visions, while compelling, were not based on any concrete scientific evidence and that her ability to foresee the future was simply a matter of chance.

Despite the skepticism, Tatsuki's renewed prediction sparked important conversations about the role of art in forecasting the future and the potential for individuals to tap into deeper truths about the world. Many began to question whether there was a deeper connection between art and reality, and whether such prophecies could provide valuable insights into the challenges humanity faces. Tatsuki's work, which had always been about more than just predicting disasters, became a symbol of the fragility of life and the importance of preparedness in the face of uncertainty.

The public's reaction to the renewed prophecy also led to increased interest in Tatsuki's earlier work, particularly The Future I Saw. Readers revisited her past predictions, searching for clues or signs that might explain how she was able to foresee such events. Her manga became a source of fascination and contemplation, as people tried to make sense of the relationship between art, prophecy, and the unfolding reality of the world.

Ultimately, the renewed prophecy about the 2025 disaster did more than just predict a potential catastrophe—it reminded people of the delicate balance between fate and free will, and the need for preparedness in a world that is constantly changing. Whether one believes in Tatsuki's ability to foresee the future or not, her work remains a thought-provoking exploration of human vulnerability and the impact of natural disasters on society. The 2025 prediction, like her earlier work, serves as a powerful reminder of the unpredictability of the world and the importance of resilience in the face of the unknown.

Chapter 6

Prophecies of the Future: Analyzing the 2025 Vision

The Science (or Lack Thereof) Behind Tatsuki's Predictions

When discussing the validity of Ryo Tatsuki's prophetic visions, one of the most pressing questions is the scientific basis (or lack thereof) behind her predictions. As a manga artist, Tatsuki's work, by its very nature, was not grounded in traditional scientific methodology or empirical research. Her predictions were not made through rigorous analysis or forecasting models; rather, they were based on her deeply personal experiences with recurring dreams—visions she claimed to have seen of the future.

While some might dismiss her abilities as coincidental or imaginative, others wonder if there could be an explanation beyond mere chance. Tatsuki's illustrations and diary entries did not involve any formal scientific tools or techniques; they were the products of her subjective experiences, influenced by her perception of the world around her. In this sense, the science behind Tatsuki's predictions is not grounded in research, data, or statistical analysis but instead emerges from her intuitive, artistic process.

However, the question remains: how could someone with no formal training in science or forecasting foresee such accurate events? Some have suggested that Tatsuki's visions may be a form of pattern recognition, where her subconscious mind picks up on subtle cues in the world and processes them in ways her conscious mind does not fully understand. This idea draws on concepts from psychology and neuroscience, where our brains are constantly processing information in the background, detecting patterns and anomalies. In this light, Tatsuki's predictions could be seen as the result of a deep, subconscious awareness of emerging trends and patterns in the world—be it political, environmental, or social—that she was able to channel through her artistic talents.

On the other hand, those who take a more skeptical view argue that Tatsuki's predictions were merely a result of random chance. They point to the inherent unpredictability of the world and suggest that the disasters she predicted were bound to occur at some point, given the cyclical nature of major events like earthquakes, tsunamis, and pandemics. By illustrating these events, Tatsuki may have simply been tapping into a common human fear and fascination with catastrophe, rather than possessing any true supernatural insight.

Ultimately, the science behind Tatsuki's predictions remains elusive. While there is no scientific evidence to support the idea that she possessed clairvoy-ant abilities, the accuracy of her predictions—particularly in the case of the Kobe earthquake, the Tōhoku disaster, and the COVID-19 pandemic—raises intriguing questions about the limits of human perception and the role that intuition and art may play in anticipating the future.

Examining the Cultural and Societal Influences on Her Prophetic Work

Ryo Tatsuki's prophetic work did not emerge in a vacuum. Her visions were shaped not only by her personal experiences but also by the cultural and societal climate in which she lived. As a Japanese artist, Tatsuki was deeply attuned to the concerns and anxieties of her society, particularly in the context of natural disasters. Japan, located on the Pacific Ring of Fire, has long been vulnerable to earthquakes, tsunamis, and volcanic eruptions. This natural landscape of seismic activity likely influenced Tatsuki's visions, as she internalized the pervasive fear of the unpredictable and destructive power of nature.

Tatsuki's predictions also reflect the broader societal anxieties of the late 20th and early 21st centuries. The 1990s and early 2000s were marked by a series of global crises, including the collapse of major economies, the threat of nuclear war, and the increasing unpredictability of climate change. These fears permeated the cultural consciousness, inspiring works of art, literature, and media that explored themes of catastrophe, loss, and the fragility of human civilization. Tatsuki's work, with its focus on global disasters and their emotional toll, can be seen as a reflection of these larger cultural trends. She was not merely creating fictional narratives but responding to the collective fears and uncertainties of her time.

Additionally, Tatsuki's visions were shaped by the social dynamics of Japan. In a country where respect for tradition and a deep sense of duty and responsibility to society are valued, the impact of major disasters like the Tōhoku earthquake and the Kobe earthquake cannot be overstated. The collective trauma experienced by the people of Japan in the aftermath of these events, coupled with the country's vulnerability to such disasters, likely influenced Tatsuki's portrayal of these catastrophes. Her predictions were not only about the physical devastation of the events themselves but about the emotional and psychological consequences for those affected. In this sense, her work is deeply connected to the Japanese experience of living with the constant threat of disaster and the emotional resilience required to rebuild in its wake.

Tatsuki's ability to tap into the societal and cultural currents of her time speaks to the way in which artists and creators often reflect and amplify the concerns of their societies. Her work is a mirror of the world around her, capturing not just the physical events but the emotions, fears, and hopes of the people who will ultimately experience them. Through her art, Tatsuki was able to distill the societal anxieties of the late 20th and early 21st centuries and transform them into a prophetic narrative that resonated deeply with her audience.

The Validity of These Predictions in the Modern Age

The question of whether Tatsuki's predictions hold validity in the modern age is a complex one. In an era dominated by science, technology, and data-driven analysis, it is difficult to reconcile her prophetic abilities with the methods we typically use to understand and forecast the future. The modern world places a premium on empirical evidence and measurable outcomes, and anything that falls outside of this framework—such as Tatsuki's seemingly supernatural visions—tends to be viewed with skepticism or dismissed as superstition.

Yet, there is a compelling case to be made for the validity of Tatsuki's predictions, even in the context of the modern age. While her visions were not based on scientific methods, they were grounded in the lived experiences of individuals and societies. Tatsuki's works were not just about predicting events—they were about capturing the emotional and psychological realities of living through them. In this way, her work resonates not just as prophecy but as a form of social and emotional commentary that speaks to the very human experience of confronting the unknown.

Moreover, the accuracy of some of her predictions—such as the Kobe earthquake, the Tōhoku disaster, and the COVID-19 pandemic—raises intriguing questions about the limits of human perception. Could it be that certain individuals, like Tatsuki, are particularly attuned to the forces shaping the future, even if they cannot explain how or why? Could her ability to see these events be the result of a heightened sensitivity to patterns or signals that the rest of society fails to notice? While this remains speculative, it is undeniable that Tatsuki's predictions have had a profound impact on those who have encountered them, prompting them to question the nature of fate, time, and human awareness.

In the modern age, where the future often feels uncertain and unpredictable, Tatsuki's prophetic work continues to serve as a powerful reminder of the importance of emotional resilience, preparedness, and the human capacity to endure in the face of crisis. Whether one views her work as a supernatural gift, a product of intense intuition, or a mere coincidence, it remains a compelling and thought-provoking exploration of the relationship between art, prophecy, and the world we inhabit. As the world continues to grapple with unprecedented challenges, Tatsuki's visions offer a unique lens through which to understand the forces that shape our collective future, reminding us that sometimes the future is not something we can predict—it is something we must be ready to face when it arrives.

Chapter 7

The Role of Art in Foreseeing the Future

Understanding How Tatsuki Used Her Artistic Abilities to Interpret Dreams

Ryo Tatsuki's prophetic work is an extraordinary blend of art, intuition, and personal experience. While many artists are known for using their creativity to reflect the world around them, Tatsuki's talent went beyond that—she used her artistic abilities to interpret her dreams and translate them into vivid, prophetic narratives. This process of interpretation was deeply personal, rooted in the recurring dreams she experienced from a young age, many of which were not mere figments of her imagination but vivid premonitions of future events. Tatsuki's artistry allowed her to channel these visions into a tangible form, capturing not only the visual aspects of the dreams but the emotions, tensions, and nuances she felt within them.

In many ways, her artistic abilities acted as a conduit for her dreams. She didn't just record what she saw in her mind's eye; she brought those visions to life with the detailed precision and emotional depth that only a skilled illustrator could achieve. Tatsuki had an uncanny ability to capture the essence of the events she foresaw, not just by drawing their physical manifestation but by embodying their emotional weight. Her illustrations conveyed the sense of uncertainty, fear, and loss that accompanied these foreseen disasters, transforming what could have been abstract concepts into something visceral and immediate. Through her art, Tatsuki communicated not only the "what" of the future but the profound "how" and "why" that made these events so impactful.

For Tatsuki, the act of creating these illustrations was as much about emotional expression as it was about prophetic communication. She often portrayed natural disasters, global tragedies, and personal losses in ways that captured the human experience in times of crisis. By using her art to bring these dreams to life, she made them tangible and real for her readers, inviting them into the world of her visions in a way that words alone could not. Through this process, Tatsuki tapped into a form of artistic expression that transcended traditional boundaries, blending her personal dreams with the larger, collective human experience of fear, resilience, and survival.

The Blending of Illustration and Prophetic Storytelling

What sets Tatsuki's work apart from other prophetic or fictional narratives is the seamless blending of illustration and storytelling. Manga, as a medium, is uniquely suited for this kind of fusion because it allows for the combination of visual elements with text in a way that no other art form can. Tatsuki took full advantage of this medium, using her illustrations not just to depict the events she foresaw, but to weave a story that was both visually stunning and deeply narrative-driven.

Her illustrations were not static images—they were integral parts of a larger narrative, one that unfolded gradually, much like the future she was trying to predict. The use of sequential art allowed Tatsuki to build tension and atmosphere in a way that isolated images alone could not achieve. She drew on the visual power of manga to convey the scope and scale of the events she predicted, whether it was a massive earthquake, a deadly virus, or a public tragedy. The fluidity of manga storytelling—its use of panels, pacing, and visual cues—enabled Tatsuki to convey the emotional arc of these events, from the calm before the storm to the devastating aftermath.

Tatsuki's prophetic storytelling also involved a careful integration of her personal experiences with universal themes. The figures in her manga were often not just symbolic representations of future events but were imbued with deeply human emotions—fear, hope, confusion, and resilience. Her characters' responses to the disasters they encountered were not merely plot devices, but reflections of how ordinary people would likely react to extraordinary circumstances. Through her art, Tatsuki offered not only a vision of the future but a profound commentary on the human condition, illustrating how individuals and communities might face and survive crises.

By blending illustration with prophetic storytelling, Tatsuki created a work that resonated on multiple levels. Her manga was more than just a series of predicted events—it was a narrative that explored the emotional, psychological, and societal impacts of those events. Through her intricate illustrations and the stories that accompanied them, Tatsuki brought her prophetic dreams to life, making the future something people could engage with and reflect upon.

How Manga as a Medium Conveys Potential Futures

Manga, as a medium, is uniquely capable of conveying potential futures in a way that is both engaging and accessible. Unlike other forms of storytelling, manga combines visual elements with narrative text, allowing for a dynamic interplay between imagery and story. This allows Tatsuki to explore her prophetic visions in a manner that is both intuitive and visually impactful, capturing the essence of the future in a way that is not just literal but emotional and psychological as well.

Manga also has a flexibility that other forms of media lack. It can be both fantastical and grounded, capable of depicting anything from otherworldly creatures to the stark realities of human life. Tatsuki used this flexibility to her advantage, crafting visions of the future that felt at once surreal and intimately familiar. Her ability to juxtapose the fantastical and the real allowed her to communicate complex ideas about fate, human resilience, and the unpredictability of life, all while grounding those ideas in events that felt both plausible and inevitable.

The visual nature of manga is another powerful tool that Tatsuki used to convey her visions of the future. By illustrating the events she foresaw in great detail, she gave her readers an almost cinematic experience of the disaster and its aftermath. The visual power of her work made her prophecies feel immediate, visceral, and real. Manga has a way of drawing readers in through its striking artwork and dynamic storytelling, which allows Tatsuki's predictions to not only be seen but felt. Her readers could experience the crushing weight of an earthquake, the chaos of a pandemic, or the sorrow of a personal loss, all through the power of her illustrations.

Manga also has a universal appeal. While Tatsuki's work was initially published in Japan, the medium's popularity has spread worldwide, making it an ideal vehicle for communicating complex ideas about the future to a global audience. The visual nature of manga transcends language barriers, allowing Tatsuki's prophetic visions to reach and resonate with readers from diverse cultural backgrounds. The global reach of manga has allowed Tatsuki's work to have a lasting impact, inviting people from all corners of the world to engage with her prophetic storytelling and reflect on the potential futures she depicted.

In this way, manga as a medium is a powerful tool for conveying not just stories, but the very essence of future possibilities. Through the interplay of art and narrative, manga allows for a fluid exploration of what might come to pass—whether it is the stark reality of a natural disaster or the emotional journey of a community facing overwhelming tragedy. Tatsuki harnessed this potential to create a body of work that spoke to the human experience, inviting readers to imagine the future and consider how they might respond to the unknown.

Tatsuki's ability to blend illustration, prophetic storytelling, and the unique qualities of the manga medium made her work not just a collection of predictions, but a deeply human exploration of what it means to face an uncertain future. Through her art, she created a bridge between dreams and reality, inviting her readers to reflect on the forces shaping the world and their place within it.

Chapter 8

Cultural Impact: From Obscurity to Global Recognition

Tatsuki's Shift from a Niche Manga Artist to a Prophetic Figure

Ryo Tatsuki's career trajectory took an unexpected and profound turn when her works, initially seen as a niche form of manga art, gained global recognition due to the accuracy of her prophetic visions. Before the widespread attention given to her predictions, Tatsuki was known primarily within the manga community for her unique storytelling style, which mixed deeply personal themes with elements of mysticism and future foresight. Her manga, The Future I Saw, was initially released with little fanfare, seen by many as just another speculative work in the crowded genre of manga storytelling.

However, Tatsuki's artistic and prophetic abilities soon set her apart. The turning point came after the 2011 Tōhoku earthquake and tsunami in Japan, when readers who had already engaged with her work began to notice the striking similarity between Tatsuki's illustrations and the real-life disaster. Her detailed depiction of the earthquake, including the massive tsunami that followed, was eerily close to the actual event that devastated northeastern Japan. As news of her "prophetic" ability spread, Tatsuki's manga shifted from a work of speculative fiction to a body of work that was taken seriously as a source of potential insight into future events.

The cultural shift that accompanied Tatsuki's rise to fame was dramatic. She went from being a relatively unknown manga artist to a figure whose works were examined, analyzed, and even revered for their foresight. Many began to view her as a prophet, someone capable of tapping into the future through her art and dreams. While Tatsuki did not claim to be a mystic or clairvoyant, the accuracy of her predictions blurred the lines between art and prophecy, and her role in Japanese culture evolved from that of an artist to that of a cultural figure whose visions were seen as having a special connection to the future.

This shift in her public perception made her an important figure in the discussion of fate, prophecy, and the unknown. As her predictions gained attention, Tatsuki's work gained a following beyond Japan. She became not just a manga artist but a global symbol of how art can capture the intangible and make the future feel more immediate and comprehensible.

The Evolution of Her Following and How Her Works Impacted Japanese Culture

Tatsuki's growing popularity marked a shift in how Japanese culture engaged with themes of prophecy, disaster, and collective anxiety. Japan, being located in the Pacific Ring of Fire, has long been familiar with the threat of natural disasters, particularly earthquakes and tsunamis. These events have shaped the national psyche, influencing everything from public policy to media representations of disaster. Tatsuki's works, particularly her prophetic predictions, resonated deeply with the Japanese people, many of whom had already experienced the trauma of past disasters, such as the 1995 Kobe earthquake.

Through her manga, Tatsuki explored the emotional and psychological impact of living with the constant threat of catastrophe. Her works tapped into a deep, collective anxiety about the unknown—about the potential for disaster to strike at any moment. Her illustrations of earthquakes, tsunamis, and pandemics were not just depictions of physical destruction; they were representations of the emotional landscape of a society living under the shadow of uncertainty. Tatsuki's ability to give form and shape to these fears made her work not just a prediction of the future but a reflection of the cultural realities faced by many Japanese people.

Tatsuki's works also sparked a broader conversation about fate, free will, and the role of art in interpreting the world. As her predictions about major global events—such as the Tōhoku earthquake and the COVID-19 pandemic— came true, her following grew exponentially. People began to turn to her work not just as a form of entertainment but as a source of insight into the future. Her ability to combine the fictional aspects of manga with the real-world implications of her visions changed the way Japanese audiences viewed the potential for art to predict or reflect the future. Tatsuki's work became a lens through which people could contemplate their place in a world that was often unpredictable and fraught with risk.

As Tatsuki's global recognition increased, so did her impact on the wider cultural landscape. Her work helped fuel a broader discussion about prophecy in modern times, prompting debates about the nature of foresight and the extent to which individuals can predict future events. Tatsuki's rise to fame coincided with the global rise of interest in alternative forms of knowledge, such as astrology, psychic phenomena, and other mystical traditions. Her ability to tap into a collective sense of fear and anticipation helped her become a key figure in this cultural shift, as more people looked to non-traditional sources of knowledge to understand the world and what might lie ahead.

The Comparison to Other Prophetic Figures Like Baba Vanga

As Tatsuki's works gained international attention, comparisons were in- evitably drawn between her and other prophetic figures, such as the Bulgarian mystic Baba Vanga. Baba Vanga, who lived from 1911 to 1996, became famous for her predictions of major global events, some of which were said to have come true. Much like Tatsuki, Baba Vanga gained a large following after her death, as people began to look back on her predictions and find connections between her visions and real-world events.

Tatsuki and Baba Vanga share certain similarities in their roles as prophetic figures. Both women were known for their ability to foresee events that were beyond the realm of conventional understanding. Baba Vanga's predictions, many of which were related to natural disasters, political upheaval, and wars, were often framed as divine revelations, while Tatsuki's visions were more personal, grounded in her dreams and artistic expression. Despite these differences in how their prophecies were framed, both women became cultural icons, their names synonymous with the idea of an individual tapping into a deeper, hidden truth about the future.

One of the key comparisons between Tatsuki and Baba Vanga lies in the public perception of their abilities. Both were seen by their followers as having a unique insight into the future, offering predictions that resonated deeply with people's concerns and anxieties about what might come next. Baba Vanga's predictions about events like the September 11 attacks and the Brexit vote gained her a cult following, while Tatsuki's accurate depictions of natural disasters, the COVID-19 pandemic, and the 2025 tsunami prediction cemented her as a prophetic figure in the modern age.

However, there are also significant differences in the way Tatsuki's work is perceived compared to Baba Vanga's. Baba Vanga's legacy is often tied to the idea of her being a mystic or clairvoyant, someone who received divine messages about the future. In contrast, Tatsuki's predictions are often framed as the result of her personal dreams and artistic process, with less emphasis on supernatural intervention. Her rise to fame is more a result of her artistic intuition and her ability to translate these visions into visual narratives, rather than an explicit claim of prophetic powers. This distinction highlights the evolving relationship between art, prophecy, and the public's understanding of the future in the modern age.

The comparison between Tatsuki and Baba Vanga also raises important questions about the nature of prophecy and the role of women in the cultural imagination. Both figures represent a challenge to traditional ideas about knowledge and foresight, offering a more intuitive, artistic interpretation of the future that resonates with a global audience. As prophetic figures, they both highlight the human need to understand and anticipate the unknown, particularly in times of crisis. Through their work, they have helped shape the modern conversation around fate, prediction, and the power of intuition in understanding the future.

Tatsuki's rise from obscurity to global recognition mirrors the broader societal interest in prophecy and alternative forms of knowledge in the 21st century. As her work continues to impact both Japanese culture and the global conversation, she stands as a testament to the power of art to convey deeper truths about the world and the forces that shape our collective future. Whether viewed as a prophet, an artist, or a cultural figure, Tatsuki's impact on contemporary culture is undeniable, and her legacy will likely continue to inspire and provoke thought for years to come.

Chapter 9

Tourism, Fear, and Prophecy: A Japan in Crisis

The Economic and Social Impact of Her 2025 Prediction on Japanese Tourism

Ryo Tatsuki's prophetic vision of a catastrophic tsunami in 2025, based on an underwater rupture between Japan and the Philippines, sent shockwaves through Japan's tourism industry and broader public consciousness. The prediction, which paints a dire picture of devastation along Japan's coastlines, especially affecting major cities, stirred a great deal of concern and uncertainty, particularly among travelers considering Japan as a destination. In the aftermath of this prophecy's resurgence in 2021, just as the world was emerging from the COVID-19 pandemic, tourism to Japan saw an immediate downturn, exacerbated by the potential threat of another natural disaster.

For Japan, a country that had already endured the trauma of the 2011 Tōhoku earthquake and tsunami, Tatsuki's renewed prediction stirred echoes of the past, reigniting fears of another disaster. Japan's tourism industry, which had been slowly recovering after COVID-19 lockdowns and travel restrictions, faced another blow. Foreign visitors, particularly those from East Asia and other disaster-prone regions, reconsidered or postponed their travel plans to Japan in light of the foreboding nature of the prophecy.

The economic implications of this renewed fear were significant. In 2019,

Japan had welcomed a record 31.9 million international visitors, marking tourism as a major industry contributing to the economy. By 2021, however, this number had dropped drastically as Tatsuki's prediction stoked fears of another catastrophic tsunami. The media frenzy surrounding her prophetic warnings further exacerbated this decline. Hotels, restaurants, and businesses dependent on international tourists found themselves facing reduced occupancy rates, while local economies in tourist hotspots like Kyoto, Tokyo, and Osaka grappled with cancellations, especially from those concerned about the safety of visiting the country in light of the 2025 tsunami prediction.

The social impact of this downturn was equally profound. Communities that thrived on tourism—both the bustling city centers and the serene rural areas—began to experience the trickle-down effects of a global decline in visitors. Workers in the hospitality and tourism sectors found themselves facing job uncertainty, with some businesses struggling to survive. For the average Japanese citizen, the heightened sense of unease led to questions about the country's future, and the risk of living under the looming threat of another natural disaster was once again brought to the forefront.

Tatsuki's prediction also caused a significant shift in how the world viewed Japan. While many saw it as a resilient country capable of recovering from past disasters, the renewed focus on the possibility of future catastrophe created a sense of vulnerability. The perceived threat of the 2025 tsunami prompted global audiences to question whether it was wise to invest in travel to Japan, given its history of seismic activity and Tatsuki's prophetic warnings.

How Speculative Predictions Influence Public Behavior

The power of speculative predictions, especially those tied to natural disasters, lies in their ability to influence public behavior—often in ways that can shape global and national markets. Tatsuki's prediction of a tsunami in 2025 had the potential to influence not only tourism but also broader behavioral shifts, as it tapped into deeply rooted fears of nature's unpredictability and the uncertain future.

Psychologically, humans have a tendency to react to fear-based information with caution, even in the absence of direct evidence. Tatsuki's prediction, while not scientifically substantiated, created a narrative that was too compelling to ignore. Even those who initially dismissed the idea of a catastrophic tsunami in 2025 found themselves reconsidering their stance when her past predictions—such as the Tōhoku earthquake and the COVID-19 pandemic—proved to be eerily accurate. This psychological effect is often referred to as the self-fulfilling prophecy, where the mere suggestion of a potential future event can lead to changes in behavior that may make the predicted event more likely, either directly or indirectly.

For tourism, the reaction was swift and tangible. As news of Tatsuki's renewed prediction spread, social media platforms buzzed with discussions about the potential for a disaster, with users sharing their concerns and speculating on the veracity of the prophecy. This led to widespread unease, particularly among travelers who had planned vacations to Japan. Fear-driven decision-making is a well-documented phenomenon, and in this case, it manifested as a drop in tourist bookings, especially for vulnerable coastal areas. Travelers may have felt that the risks of visiting Japan outweighed the rewards, given the potential for another tsunami to wreak havoc on the country.

Moreover, Tatsuki's predictions played into broader societal anxieties. As global crises, including natural disasters, pandemics, and political upheaval, continued to dominate headlines, many people began to view her predictions as more than mere coincidence. For individuals who were already on edge due to the uncertainties of the modern world, Tatsuki's warnings felt like a tangible reminder of the fragility of life. This sense of vulnerability often leads to avoidance behavior, whether it's in the form of avoiding certain regions, altering travel plans, or making changes to daily routines to mitigate perceived risks.

Tatsuki's work, blending prophecy with art, tapped into this universal sense of fear and uncertainty. The prediction about the tsunami in 2025 was, for many, more than just a potential disaster—it became a symbol of the unknown. And as history has shown, people's reactions to uncertainty often lead to avoidance, withdrawal, or preemptive caution, which can ripple through markets and industries, leaving lasting effects on public behavior.

The Role of the Government in Mitigating Fear and Uncertainty

In the face of Tatsuki's renewed prophecy and the resulting public fear, the role of the Japanese government in mitigating uncertainty and protecting the tourism industry became crucial. The Japanese government, which had worked tirelessly to rebuild and recover after the 2011 Tōhoku earthquake and tsunami, had to respond quickly to address both the economic and emotional fallout from the resurgence of disaster-related fears. Ensuring the safety of its citizens and visitors while maintaining Japan's reputation as a resilient and welcoming destination was key to Japan's recovery.

One of the government's most important tasks was to provide a clear, scientific response to the prophecy. Japan has long been at the forefront of seismic research, with its government investing heavily in technologies designed to predict and mitigate the impact of earthquakes and tsunamis. In response to Tatsuki's prediction, officials reaffirmed Japan's commitment to disaster preparedness and safety measures, reassuring the public and international tourists that the government had the infrastructure in place to respond to any potential future disaster. The Japan Meteorological Agency (JMA), in particular, became a key player in combating the narrative of impending doom, emphasizing that while Japan is at risk for seismic activity, its disaster preparedness systems remain one of the most advanced in the world.

Public reassurance also came in the form of disaster preparedness campaigns aimed at educating citizens and tourists alike about the steps they could take to protect themselves. These campaigns included everything from tsunami evacuation drills to information about Japan's early warning systems. The government also sought to highlight the measures in place to keep visitors safe, such as updated building codes and evacuation routes for tourists staying in coastal areas. These proactive steps helped to counterbalance the fear generated by the 2025 prediction, providing the public with a sense of control and safety in the face of potential uncertainty.

Moreover, the Japanese government worked closely with the tourism industry to mitigate the economic impact of the prophecy on tourism. The Ministry of Land, Infrastructure, Transport and Tourism (MLIT) launched a series of promotional campaigns emphasizing Japan's cultural and historical attractions, focusing on regions less vulnerable to tsunamis. This shift in marketing helped to divert attention away from coastal areas while encouraging visitors to explore the rich cultural heritage of inland cities like Kyoto, Nara, and Hiroshima.

The government also collaborated with international travel agencies to reassure global tourists that Japan remains a safe and vibrant destination, emphasizing the country's ability to recover from past disasters and maintain a secure environment for travelers. In this way, the government sought to strike a delicate balance between acknowledging the reality of natural disaster risks and reassuring the public about the ongoing safety measures in place.

The economic and social impact of Tatsuki's 2025 tsunami prediction underscored the fragile relationship between public perception and global tourism. While speculative predictions can shape public behavior, the government's role in managing fear, uncertainty, and public perception became essential in mitigating the fallout from such prophecies. By combining proactive disaster preparedness efforts with strategic communication, Japan was able to stabilize its tourism sector and maintain its position as a leading global destination, despite the fear-driven decline in tourism following the prophecy's resurgence. The episode illustrates not only the power of art and prophecy in shaping public consciousness but also the resilience of societies in the face of uncertainty.

Chapter 10

Prophecy and Skepticism: The Debate Between Belief and Science

The Tension Between Prophetic Visions and Scientific Explanations

The tension between prophetic visions and scientific explanations is at the heart of the debate surrounding Ryo Tatsuki's predictions. On one hand, we have the realm of scientific inquiry, which is grounded in evidence, logic, and empirical research, and on the other, the realm of prophecy, which relies on intuition, dreams, and often unverifiable visions of the future. Tatsuki's works, which have been heralded by some as eerily accurate glimpses into future disasters, sit in a space between these two realms, provoking deep questions about how we understand the unknown.

From a scientific perspective, predictions about the future are typically based on the study of observable data, trends, and probabilities. Scientists rely on theories, models, and repeatable experiments to forecast outcomes. For example, the prediction of a potential tsunami is based on the understanding of tectonic plate movements, the study of past seismic activity, and advanced warning systems. Such predictions are rooted in observable and quantifiable data, ensuring a certain degree of reliability.

Tatsuki's prophetic work, in contrast, operates outside the scientific method. Her visions are personal, subjective, and not derived from traditional data-driven approaches. While her predictions—such as the 2011 Tōhoku earth-quake and the COVID-19 pandemic—may appear to have been uncannily accurate, they were not based on scientific evidence but on intuitive dreams and artistic interpretation. This creates a fundamental challenge for those who view the world through a scientific lens: how do we reconcile these two seemingly incompatible forms of knowledge—one grounded in empirical data, the other in the realm of personal insight and foresight?

The difficulty arises when trying to explain how a non-scientific person like Tatsuki could foresee specific, catastrophic events. Science, by its very nature, relies on the belief that the world follows predictable patterns, driven by observable forces. Prophecy, however, operates in a realm where the unknown and the unpredictable are paramount. Where science offers certainty, prophecy offers possibility—and that uncertainty can be both compelling and unsettling.

How Skeptics and Believers Interpret Tatsuki's Works

The divide between skeptics and believers in Tatsuki's work is a natural outcome of the tension between belief and science. Those who approach her work with skepticism often point out that the events she predicted could be classified as "vague" or "generic." For example, earthquakes, tsunamis, and pandemics are all natural occurrences that have happened throughout history. In a world constantly exposed to news about natural disasters and health crises, critics argue, the prediction of such events could easily be seen as playing on universal fears or making broad statements that have a high probability of coming true at some point.

Skeptics also argue that Tatsuki's work falls within the realm of confirma-tion bias—the tendency for people to remember predictions that come true and disregard those that don't. They point to the fact that, like many other prophetic figures, Tatsuki may have made numerous predictions that did not come to pass. In this view, the seeming accuracy of her visions is simply a product of selective attention: when a disaster occurs that aligns with one of her predictions, it reinforces the belief that she had some supernatural insight.

Conversely, when predictions do not materialize, they are either forgotten or dismissed.

Moreover, skeptics often question the method through which Tatsuki makes her predictions—through dreams and personal visions—arguing that these are products of subconscious thoughts rather than foresight. Dreams are known to be highly symbolic, often reflecting internal fears, anxieties, and desires. In this interpretation, Tatsuki's dreams are no different from those of any other person, and the accuracy of her predictions could simply be the result of her unconscious mind picking up on subtle cues in the environment that were then reflected in her dreams.

On the other hand, believers interpret Tatsuki's work through a lens of faith and mysticism. They view her ability to foresee future events as a gift or a manifestation of a deeper connection to the world's underlying truths. For many, Tatsuki's work resonates because it offers a sense of certainty in an unpredictable world—her predictions provide a roadmap of sorts, offering glimpses of what may come and thus giving individuals a sense of control over their futures. Believers argue that the events she predicted, such as the 1995 Kobe earthquake, the Tōhoku disaster, and the COVID-19 pandemic, were not random occurrences but part of a broader, interconnected reality that Tatsuki had tapped into.

For believers, Tatsuki's work is a reminder that there are forces in the universe beyond our understanding, forces that art and intuition can sometimes access. They view her work as a bridge between the material world and the spiritual or metaphysical realm. The accuracy of her predictions, they argue, is proof that there is something more to human perception than what can be observed with the naked eye or understood through traditional scientific methods. In this context, Tatsuki's predictions are not seen as coincidences, but as expressions of a deeper, often hidden, truth about the nature of reality.

Case Studies of Other Notable Prophetic Predictions

Tatsuki's work inevitably draws comparisons to other famous prophetic figures, whose predictions have had similar cultural impacts. One of the most well-known of these figures is Baba Vanga, the Bulgarian mystic who is often credited with foreseeing major world events, including the 9/11 attacks, the rise of ISIS, and the Brexit referendum. Like Tatsuki, Baba Vanga became a symbol of prophecy, gaining a global following of believers who pointed to her accuracy as evidence of her supernatural abilities. However, as with Tatsuki, her predictions were often vague and open to interpretation, and many critics argue that her "visions" were nothing more than a series of coincidental alignments with real-world events.

Another example is Nostradamus, the 16th-century French astrologer whose quatrains have been interpreted as predictions of events ranging from the French Revolution to the rise of Adolf Hitler and the September 11 attacks. Nostradamus, much like Tatsuki, was a figure whose work has been reexamined throughout history to find correlations with contemporary events. However, skeptics argue that his quatrains were so vague and cryptic that they could be interpreted in many different ways, and any resemblance to real-world events is merely a product of retrospective interpretation.

In the 20th century, figures like Edgar Cayce, often called the "Sleeping Prophet," also gained attention for their visions of the future. Cayce, who entered a trance-like state to provide psychic readings, made predictions about future global events, including a predicted future rise of global diseases, that have since been revisited by some as eerily accurate. While some of his predictions have been validated by later events, others have not materialized, leading critics to suggest that his readings were a combination of common sense and the human tendency to see patterns where none exist.

In all of these cases, the line between prophecy and coincidence is a blurry one. Critics argue that such predictions are often general, ambiguous, and open to interpretation, meaning they can be applied to a wide range of situations. For believers, however, the accuracy of these predictions—whether they concern natural disasters, political upheaval, or health crises—is taken as evidence of a deeper, hidden truth about the world that science and reason cannot explain.

The key difference between Tatsuki and figures like Baba Vanga and Nostradamus is that Tatsuki's work is primarily artistic, with a focus on conveying the emotional and psychological impact of the future rather than providing clear, prescriptive visions of specific events. While her predictions may be open to interpretation, they are rooted in personal experience and artistic expression, rather than the mystical or esoteric traditions that underpinned the work of figures like Baba Vanga and Nostradamus.

The Debate Between Belief and Science

The debate between belief and science in the context of Ryo Tatsuki's work underscores the broader tension between empirical knowledge and subjective experience. For skeptics, Tatsuki's work represents an intersection of coincidence, selective attention, and the human tendency to find patterns in the world. For believers, her predictions offer a glimpse into a deeper, more intuitive understanding of the future, where art and intuition have the power to unveil truths that scientific methods may never fully grasp.

In the end, Tatsuki's work challenges us to reconsider the role of prophecy, art, and intuition in our understanding of the world. Whether one views her predictions as coincidental or prophetic, they serve as a reminder of how deeply human the search for answers to the future truly is, and how, sometimes, the answers may lie not in data or logic, but in the unseen realms of dreams, art, and imagination.

Chapter 11

A New Age of Prophecy: The Future of Tatsuki's Legacy

What Lies Ahead for Ryo Tatsuki's Influence on Art and Prophecy

Ryo Tatsuki's influence on art and prophecy extends far beyond her initial emergence as a niche manga artist. Her blend of personal visions and artistic storytelling has carved out a unique space for her in the cultural landscape, positioning her as not just an artist but a prophetic figure whose works tap into deep societal fears, collective anxieties, and the human search for meaning in the face of uncertainty. As her past predictions— such as the Tōhoku earthquake, the COVID-19 pandemic, and other global disasters—continue to resonate with readers, Tatsuki's legacy is poised to remain influential in the years ahead.

Looking to the future, Tatsuki's influence is likely to continue to shape the way we think about prophecy and art. Her work has already demonstrated the power of art to evoke deep emotional and psychological responses to foreseen events, and this could expand into broader artistic movements that seek to engage with the future in a similar way. The intersection of prophecy and art is likely to become a more prominent theme as global crises—be it in the form of environmental disasters, political upheaval, or health crises—continue to challenge societies worldwide. Artists, writers, and creators may increasingly turn to Tatsuki's model of using visual storytelling to engage with the potential futures of humanity, blending elements of intuition, emotional resonance, and predictive storytelling.

Tatsuki's legacy may also pave the way for a more nuanced understanding of prophecy in the modern world. Her ability to create powerful, emotional narratives based on personal visions shows that prophecy need not be framed purely in terms of predictions or cold, scientific forecasts. Instead, prophecy in the 21st century may become more about grappling with the psychological, social, and emotional dimensions of the unknown, inviting people to reflect on how they respond to potential futures. Just as Tatsuki used her dreams to reflect on the broader human experience, future generations of creators may continue to use art as a tool for understanding and interpreting an increasingly complex world.

How Modern Culture Engages with Prophetic Narratives

In the modern world, prophetic narratives have found a new home within popular culture, particularly in the realms of film, literature, and digital media. From apocalyptic science fiction to speculative dystopias, prophetic stories have captivated audiences for decades, reflecting society's deep-seated fears about the future. These narratives often explore the fragility of civilization and the unpredictability of global events, themes that resonate with people living in an era marked by political instability, climate change, and pandemics.

Ryo Tatsuki's work fits squarely within this cultural framework. Her ability to predict catastrophic events, through the medium of manga, taps into the same anxieties that drive modern apocalyptic storytelling. But while many prophetic narratives in popular culture focus on dystopian futures or grand, world-altering events, Tatsuki's works engage with the personal and emotional consequences of these predictions. Her focus on the human experience—how individuals and societies cope with the fallout of disaster—speaks to a deeper, more intimate concern with the future. In a world where technology, social media, and digital communication constantly expose us to both real and imagined crises, Tatsuki's prophetic visions offer an emotional connection to future events that is rarely explored in mainstream culture.

Furthermore, Tatsuki's use of manga—a medium that combines visual art with narrative storytelling—allows her to engage with prophetic narratives in a way that resonates with younger generations, who are increasingly drawn to graphic novels, webcomics, and other visual forms of storytelling. This makes Tatsuki's work uniquely positioned to continue influencing the way people interact with prophetic themes in a rapidly changing world. As manga and graphic novels continue to rise in popularity worldwide, her influence may continue to grow, especially as creators seek to explore the boundaries between art, prophecy, and the human experience of the future.

Social media and digital platforms also play a crucial role in shaping how modern audiences engage with prophetic narratives. With the rise of internet culture, online communities are able to instantly share and discuss ideas, predictions, and creative works. Tatsuki's work, particularly her 2025 tsunami prediction, is an example of how the internet accelerates the dissemination of ideas, allowing for rapid public discourse around potentially prophetic events. In the age of viral content, where information (and misinformation) spreads quickly, the role of prophetic narratives—whether in art, literature, or online forums—becomes more relevant than ever. Tatsuki's work may inspire not only future creators but also online communities that discuss and interpret potential future events, further blurring the lines between art, culture, and prophecy.

A Look at the Ongoing Relevance of Her Predictions in a Rapidly Changing World

As the world continues to grapple with unprecedented challenges—climate change, pandemics, political unrest, and economic instability—Tatsuki's predictions take on a new level of relevance. While her works were initially met with skepticism, her accurate foresight of past global events lends her a certain gravitas in today's world. Her depictions of natural disasters, societal collapse, and collective trauma resonate strongly in the context of the world's ongoing struggles with environmental and health crises.

For instance, Tatsuki's vision of the 2025 tsunami serves as a poignant reminder of the fragility of coastal cities in the Pacific Ring of Fire, where seismic activity and the threat of tsunamis are constant concerns. As the world becomes increasingly aware of the environmental impact of human activity—especially in terms of climate change and natural resource depletion—the question of whether we are prepared for future disasters grows ever more urgent. Tatsuki's prophetic narrative, which touches on the emotional and psychological toll of facing an uncertain future, speaks to the growing global awareness of the need for disaster preparedness and resilience.

In addition to natural disasters, Tatsuki's ability to foresee the societal impact of global events is particularly relevant in today's world. The COVID-19 pandemic, which Tatsuki predicted years before it occurred, demonstrated the vulnerability of global health systems and the interconnectedness of nations. The widespread fear, isolation, and economic turmoil caused by the pandemic mirrored the emotional landscape Tatsuki depicted in her prophetic works. As the world continues to face new health threats, political instability, and social unrest, Tatsuki's work offers a powerful lens through which to examine the human experience of uncertainty, crisis, and recovery.

Moreover, her work speaks to the growing global recognition of the need for mental health support in the wake of crises. In her depictions of disaster and trauma, Tatsuki focused not just on the physical destruction but also on the psychological scars left behind. As mental health becomes an increasingly important topic in global discourse, Tatsuki's work serves as a poignant reminder of the emotional resilience required to survive a world that is often unpredictable and fraught with risk.

In a rapidly changing world, where technology is evolving at an unprecedented pace and new challenges emerge daily, Tatsuki's predictions continue to resonate with a global audience that is coming to terms with the uncertainties of the future. Her works are not just relics of a past era but timely explorations of the human spirit in times of crisis, offering insights into how individuals and societies can cope with the unknown.

As the world enters a new age of uncertainty, Ryo Tatsuki's prophetic work remains highly relevant. Her unique ability to blend art, intuition, and storytelling has created a legacy that speaks to both the personal and societal dimensions of prophecy. Her predictions, while rooted in the realm of dreams

54

and personal visions, continue to inspire and provoke thought in a world increasingly defined by crises. Whether viewed as a prophecy, a work of art, or a cultural commentary, Tatsuki's legacy will likely endure, influencing future generations of creators, readers, and thinkers as they navigate an unpredictable world.

Chapter 12

What We Choose to Believe

Reflecting on the Implications of Tatsuki's Predictions

R yo Tatsuki's prophetic predictions have left an indelible mark on both the art world and the cultural landscape. Whether viewed as premonitions, art, or a combination of both, her visions of future events—earthquakes, pandemics, and societal crises—have sparked both awe and skepticism. The key to understanding Tatsuki's legacy lies not necessarily in whether her predictions were scientifically or metaphysically "true," but in the way her work challenges us to engage with the future. Her art forces us to reflect on how we understand the unknown and the uncertain, and how we, as individuals and societies, prepare for what lies ahead.

Tatsuki's visions have always been more than simple forecasts—they are windows into the emotional and psychological landscape of humanity in the face of disaster. Her work portrays not just the inevitable collapse of buildings or systems, but the deep, personal impact such events have on individuals. The grief, the fear, the hope, and the resilience that her characters express in the wake of her predicted disasters provide a compelling narrative about the human condition in times of crisis. In this way, Tatsuki's predictions offer an invitation: to reflect on how we, as individuals, relate to the future, and to consider how prepared we are for the unexpected.

The implications of Tatsuki's predictions also highlight the way in which art can shape our understanding of the future. Her ability to forecast significant events challenges the conventional boundary between artistic imagination and real-world impact. Whether through the lens of prophecy or art, Tatsuki's work opens up questions about how the future is imagined, interpreted, and communicated. It prompts us to consider the power of stories—particularly those based on foresight or intuition—to affect how we perceive the world and our place within it.

The Role of Individual Agency in Shaping Future Events

Tatsuki's work ultimately speaks to the power of individual agency in shaping future events. While her prophetic predictions certainly resonate on a collective level, they also suggest that how we respond to potential future crises plays a crucial role in the outcomes we experience. In her depictions of disasters, the true impact is not solely the physical destruction of buildings or cities; it is the emotional resilience and actions of individuals who navigate these events. Her characters' ability to adapt, rebuild, and heal provides an essential lesson in agency.

The future, as presented in Tatsuki's work, is not a rigid, pre-determined path but a fluid space where individual choices matter. Each person's reaction to disaster—whether it is one of fear, perseverance, or unity—contributes to how society as a whole moves forward. In a world where disasters, whether natural or man-made, seem increasingly frequent, Tatsuki's work reminds us that we have the power to shape our own response. The personal and collective choices we make in times of crisis can either amplify or mitigate the effects of the events we face.

This idea of agency is particularly pertinent in the context of today's global challenges, where we are confronted with not only natural disasters but also social and environmental crises. While we cannot control the unfolding of events, we can influence how we prepare, respond, and ultimately recover. Tatsuki's work, with its focus on emotional resilience, suggests that the most important factor in facing an uncertain future is not the event itself but how we choose to meet it. Our capacity for adaptation, empathy, and collective action will ultimately determine how we navigate the complexities of the future.

Closing Thoughts on Prophecy, Art, and the Unknown

As we close this reflection on Tatsuki's work and its place in contemporary culture, we are left with fundamental questions about prophecy, art, and the unknown. Tatsuki's blend of artistic expression and prophetic insight challenges traditional boundaries, forcing us to reconsider the role of art in not just reflecting the world, but in anticipating and interpreting the future. Her ability to create vivid, emotionally charged narratives about potential disasters invites us to engage with the unknown not as a distant, abstract concept, but as something immediate and personal.

Prophecy, in this context, is not necessarily about predicting specific events with precision, but about providing a lens through which to explore human responses to the unknown. Art, like Tatsuki's, allows us to process our collective fears, anxieties, and hopes, and to imagine how we might navigate a world that is often unpredictable and fraught with risk. It is a space where we can confront the uncertainties of the future with a sense of agency and awareness, as well as a deep understanding of the emotional and psychological toll these events take on us.

Tatsuki's legacy reminds us that prophecy and art are not mutually exclusive but can coexist as powerful tools for exploring the future. Through her work, we are invited to reflect on the nature of fate and free will, on the role of art in shaping public consciousness, and on the power of individual agency to transform the course of events. The future may remain uncertain, but it is through our engagement with art, our understanding of the past, and our actions in the present that we can begin to shape the unknown into something we can navigate together.

In the end, what we choose to believe, whether in the power of prophetic visions, the certainty of scientific analysis, or the emotional resonance of art, will shape the way we experience the future. Tatsuki's work, with its deep emotional insight and vivid depictions of potential futures, challenges us to think more critically about how we engage with the unknown and how we

58

can collectively respond to the crises that lie ahead. In doing so, she leaves behind a legacy that goes beyond prophecy—it is an invitation to embrace the unknown with both caution and hope, ready to face whatever may come.

APPENDICES

Appendix A: Overview of Ryo Tatsuki's Works

A **Comprehensive List of Tatsuki's Manga and Other Artistic Projects** Ryo Tatsuki's body of work spans several decades, and her impact on the world of manga and prophetic art is profound. While she is best known for The Future I Saw (が た, Watashi ga Mita Mirai), Tatsuki's portfolio includes a variety of manga, illustrations, and other artistic projects that have cemented her reputation as both an artist and a visionary. Here is a comprehensive list of Tatsuki's most notable works:

1. The Future I Saw (が た)

- Release Year: 1999 (Reprint in 2021)
- Genre: Prophetic, Science Fiction, Drama
- Synopsis: This manga is Tatsuki's most famous work, where she depicts a series of prophetic dreams and visions, each detailing significant global disasters—such as earthquakes, pandemics, and public tragedies. Through a mixture of haunting illustrations and deeply personal storytelling, Tatsuki foresees major world events, drawing from her own dreams and inner reflections on the human experience of disaster.

2. Fragments of Tomorrow (の, Ashita no Kakera)

- Release Year: 2004

- Genre: Psychological Thriller, Drama
- Synopsis: This lesser-known work explores the theme of fate and free will through a series of interconnected short stories. Each narrative examines how small, seemingly insignificant choices shape the trajectories of individual lives, offering insights into how one's actions may unknowingly contribute to future outcomes.

3. Visions of the Unseen (えざるビジョン, Miezaru Bijon)

- Release Year: 2007
- Genre: Supernatural, Mystery
- Synopsis: In Visions of the Unseen, Tatsuki explores the blurry line between dreams and reality, following the story of a young woman who begins to experience vivid premonitions of future events. As she grapples with the growing fear of what is to come, the narrative delves into themes of perception, control, and the psychological toll of foresight.

4. Echoes of Time (のき, Toki no Hibiki)

- Release Year: 2013
- Genre: Historical Fiction, Drama
- Synopsis: This work is a departure from Tatsuki's usual apocalyptic themes, instead focusing on historical events through the lens of a fictional narrative. Set in Japan during the Meiji Restoration, Echoes of Time tells the story of a young samurai caught between tradition and modernity, exploring the concept of fate in the context of societal transformation.

5. Whispers from the Void (からのき, Kyomu kara no Sasayaki)

- Release Year: 2016
- Genre: Horror, Psychological Drama
- Synopsis: In this unsettling manga, Tatsuki explores the psychological

horror of encountering the unknown. The story centers on a group of people who, after experiencing a collective traumatic event, begin to hear strange voices from the future, each whispering terrifying predictions of doom.

6. The Dreaming World (る, Yume Miru Sekai)

- Release Year: 2019
- Genre: Science Fiction, Fantasy, Adventure
- Synopsis: Tatsuki's foray into science fiction, The Dreaming World imagines a future where humanity has colonized distant planets and must confront the consequences of tampering with time. Blending speculative fiction with her trademark exploration of emotional resilience, this work deals with the unintended consequences of humanity's desire to control time itself.

Discussion on the Themes, Styles, and Evolution of Her Work

Ryo Tatsuki's works are deeply influenced by her personal experiences with dreams, intuition, and the human desire to understand and prepare for the future. A consistent theme throughout her work is the exploration of fate and free will—how individuals and societies respond to predestined events. While Tatsuki's stories often depict grand, world-changing disasters, they are equally focused on the emotional toll these events take on individuals. Whether it's the shock of an earthquake, the isolation of a pandemic, or the psychological fallout from tragedy, her characters often undergo a journey of resilience and adaptation.

Tatsuki's artistic style evolved over the years, shifting from more traditional manga aesthetics to incorporate surreal, abstract elements that reflect the psychological and emotional aspects of her narratives. Her early works, like The Future I Saw, were marked by sharp lines and realistic proportions, creating a stark contrast between the ordinary world and the extraordinary, catastrophic events she depicted. As her work progressed, her style grew more expressive, with more fluid, dreamlike illustrations that blurred the line between reality and premonition. This shift in style mirrors her evolving understanding of the future—not as a rigid path, but as a series of interconnected possibilities that are both fluid and uncertain.

Tatsuki's writing is notable for its emotional depth and psychological realism. Her characters are often caught in moments of profound personal crisis as they come to terms with the reality of an unknowable future. Whether the disaster is a natural event, a health crisis, or a societal collapse, Tatsuki's work is a deep exploration of the human spirit and its capacity to survive in the face of the unknown.

Evolution of Themes: Early works like The Future I Saw focused largely on prophetic visions of disaster, while her later projects, such as Echoes of Time and Visions of the Unseen, broadened her exploration to include psychological, emotional, and historical dimensions. Over time, Tatsuki's focus shifted from simply predicting events to delving deeper into how these events affect the psyche of individuals and communities. In her later works, such as The Dreaming World, there is also an increasing focus on the consequences of humanity's actions—not just in the realm of natural disaster, but in the realm of technology, society, and human relationships.

Insights into Her Influences and the Reception of Her Work Over Time

Ryo Tatsuki's work has been influenced by a variety of cultural and artistic traditions, both within Japan and internationally. Her early exposure to traditional Japanese art forms, including ukiyo-e (woodblock prints) and Japanese horror manga, shaped her visual style and narrative sensibility. Her deep understanding of emotional storytelling, influenced by the works of authors like Haruki Murakami and Yukio Mishima, allowed her to craft complex characters who are not merely passive witnesses to disasters but active participants in their own emotional and psychological journeys.

Tatsuki's prophetic works also share similarities with other visionary artists and mystics, such as Baba Vanga and Nostradamus, whose works have sparked both fascination and skepticism. However, Tatsuki's art is unique in that it places significant emphasis on the human experience in times of crisis, focusing not only on the predictions themselves but on the psychological, societal, and emotional aftermath of such predictions.

The reception of Tatsuki's work has evolved significantly over time. Initially, she was recognized primarily within the manga community, with The Future I Saw garnering attention from readers who were interested in her ability to blend art with visionary themes. However, after the Tōhoku earthquake and her subsequent predictions of the COVID-19 pandemic, Tatsuki's works gained global recognition, particularly in the realm of prophetic art. Her ability to predict such specific events led to widespread media attention and the growth of her fanbase, not only in Japan but internationally.

While some critics continue to view Tatsuki's predictions with skepticism, many have come to appreciate her artistic prowess and the emotional depth of her work. Her unique combination of prophecy and art has earned her a place in the broader cultural conversation about how art, intuition, and foresight intersect in a world that is increasingly defined by uncertainty.

Ryo Tatsuki's legacy as both an artist and a prophetic figure continues to evolve. Her works remain a powerful exploration of fate, resilience, and the human spirit, and they offer a unique lens through which to view both the known and the unknown aspects of the world. As global events continue to unfold, Tatsuki's predictions—whether understood as art, prophecy, or a combination of both—will undoubtedly continue to inspire reflection, discussion, and debate.

Appendix B: Understanding Prophecy in Art

A Guide to the Intersection of Prophecy and Art Across Various Cultures

Throughout history, art has often served as a means for individuals to express and explore the future—whether through dreams, visions, or a keen understanding of the world around them. The intersection of prophecy and art has taken many forms across different cultures, with prophetic visions often becoming a central aspect of artistic expression. Whether through the depictions of ancient prophets, mystical visions, or future predictions, artists have played a significant role in interpreting and reflecting the unknown.

1. Ancient Civilizations and Prophetic Art

In ancient civilizations, the connection between art and prophecy was often seen as divinely inspired. Artists would create visual representations of gods, spiritual realms, and the future as a way of communicating with deities or spirits. Ancient Egyptian art, for example, often depicted the future in the form of afterlife scenes, offering glimpses into the journey beyond death. These depictions were not merely artistic; they were symbolic of what was to come after life, providing a form of prophecy about the spiritual journey.

Similarly, in ancient Greek and Roman art, mythology and visions of the future were central themes. Prophets, oracles, and seers were often depicted in works that explored their ability to foresee events. The most famous example is the Oracle of Delphi, whose prophecies were often immortalized in art and literature. The concept of fate was a major aspect of ancient culture, and art served as a means to illustrate this idea—depicting future events as a series of inevitable outcomes guided by divine will.

2. Religious and Mystical Art

In the Middle Ages, religious art often took on a prophetic role. The Christian tradition, in particular, saw visions of the future depicted in illuminated manuscripts, frescoes, and altarpieces. The Book of Revelation, with its vivid imagery of the end times, has been a frequent subject of prophetic art. Artists like Hieronymus Bosch created works that illustrated apocalyptic themes, offering a visual representation of the prophecies found in religious texts. These pieces were not just artistic expressions; they were tools for contemplation, allowing viewers to reflect on the future of humanity through the lens of spirituality.

In other religious traditions, such as Islamic art, Hinduism, and Buddhism, visions of future enlightenment or cosmic events were also depicted through sacred art. These representations were less concerned with specific events and more focused on spiritual prophecy—visions of peace, rebirth, and the unfolding of divine will. Here, prophecy in art was not merely about predicting material events but about communicating metaphysical truths about the universe and humanity's place within it.

3. Modern Interpretations of Prophecy in Art

In more recent centuries, the role of prophecy in art has evolved to include personal visions, social commentary, and reflections on the future of civilization. The Romantic period, with artists like William Blake and Caspar David Friedrich, was a time when the supernatural and the unknown began to emerge as central themes in art. Blake, for instance, integrated prophetic visions into his poetry and illustrations, imagining a world where divine forces shaped history and human destiny.

In the 20th century, art began to address more material and contemporary forms of prophecy, with artists reflecting on the future through political, social, and environmental lenses. Dystopian fiction, including works like George Orwell's 1984 and Aldous Huxley's Brave New World, sparked new forms of art that predicted future societal collapse, technological overreach, and the loss of individual freedoms. Artists responded with visual interpretations of these themes, capturing the anxieties of a rapidly changing world.

The use of art as prophecy is now increasingly tied to cultural reflection, where art serves as both a critique of present conditions and a speculative vision of the future.

How Artists Have Historically Used Their Work to Predict or Reflect on the Future

Artistic predictions of the future have been as much about reflection as they have been about foretelling. Many artists throughout history have used their works to speculate on future societal developments, often blending their imagination with the current state of the world. Art allows for an exploration of what might be, either through symbolic imagery, surrealistic depictions, or allegorical narratives.

1. Surrealism and the Unknown

Surrealist artists like Salvador Dalí and René Magritte were not prophetic in the traditional sense of foreseeing disasters, but they created works that questioned the nature of reality and time. Through their use of dream-like imagery and distorted perceptions, they explored the unknown aspects of human consciousness. This exploration of the subconscious and the future of human thought in a rapidly changing world reflected an understanding that the future would not be a straightforward progression but would be shaped by forces outside of our comprehension.

2. Political and Social Commentary

66

In the early 20th century, artists like Diego Rivera and Pablo Picasso began using their works as social commentary, reflecting on the political and social future of their time. Rivera's murals, for example, were both a critique of contemporary society and a visionary depiction of the potential for change. Art became a tool for warning about the consequences of unchecked industrialization, political oppression, and the threat of war. These works were intended to inspire action and change, but they also served as a form of artistic prophecy, offering a glimpse into the potential futures shaped by human behavior.

3. Science Fiction and Speculative Art

In the mid-20th century, the rise of science fiction and speculative fiction in literature was matched by a surge in visual art that reflected these imagined futures. Artists like Chris Foss, who illustrated science fiction book covers, and Moebius, known for his work in comics, used their art to depict worlds that were both futuristic and cautionary. Their works often explored the implications of technological advancements, alien contact, and environmental destruction. In many ways, these artists were acting as modern-day prophets, offering visual representations of possible futures shaped by human progress, or the lack thereof.

4. Digital Art and the Future of Technology

As technology and artificial intelligence continue to evolve, contemporary artists are grappling with the implications of a future dominated by digital advancements. Artists working with virtual reality and AI-generated art are increasingly exploring themes of transhumanism and machine learning. The art produced today is deeply reflective of the technological trajectory that human society is on, with works often depicting dystopian futures, AI uprisings, or a world where humanity has merged with technology.

A Deeper Dive into the Role of Intuition and Creativity in Shaping Prophetic Narratives

At the heart of prophetic art is intuition—the ability to sense and interpret the unseen. This intuition is not always rooted in logical reasoning but is often a subconscious process through which artists tap into deeper truths or feelings that transcend the observable world. Prophetic artists like Tatsuki,

Blake, and Dalí were able to channel their inner visions to create works that not only reflect the present but offer a glimpse into what might be.

The role of creativity in prophetic narratives is equally crucial. While intuition provides the raw material, creativity allows it to take shape, translating abstract feelings and visions into something tangible and communicable. Through their work, artists interpret the intangible aspects of the future— whether it's a prediction of a disaster, a societal shift, or an emotional journey. In this way, art becomes a bridge between the known and the unknown, offering a pathway to understand and confront future possibilities.

For artists like Tatsuki, creativity allows for the exploration of personal visions, which then resonate with larger cultural anxieties. Her ability to visualize and communicate her dreams about the future demonstrates how artists use creativity to engage with what cannot be seen—whether it is through symbols, allegory, or surreal imagery. This role of creativity in shaping prophecy highlights that art is not just about reflecting the world as it is, but about imagining and interpreting the world as it could be.

In the realm of prophetic art, intuition and creativity are intertwined, giving rise to visions of the future that, while speculative, offer insight into the emotional and psychological dimensions of potential events. These works serve as both a reflection of present-day anxieties and a guide for navigating an uncertain future, making art a powerful tool for understanding the world that is yet to come.

Appendix C: The Science of Prophetic Predictions

A Breakdown of Scientific Perspectives on Premonitions, Intuition, and Pattern Recognition

In examining the science of prophetic predictions, it is essential to differentiate between the intuitive and the empirical. Prophecies—especially those like Ryo Tatsuki's, which arise from dreams, visions, or intuitive insights—often provoke significant debate because they challenge conventional scientific understandings of how we predict or forecast events. From a scientific standpoint, what is often labeled as "prophecy" may be interpreted as

68

a complex interplay of intuition, pattern recognition, and subconscious processing of information.

1. Premonitions and Intuition

Premonitions are experiences in which an individual has a sense or feeling that an event will occur in the future, even when no explicit evidence exists. While science does not support the concept of supernatural foresight, many psychologists believe that intuition plays a role in what may appear to be prophetic visions. Intuition is the brain's ability to process vast amounts of information rapidly, often without conscious awareness. This processing happens through pattern recognition, a cognitive function that allows the brain to recognize familiar patterns and predict likely outcomes, based on previous experiences and knowledge.

From a neuroscientific perspective, intuition is often the result of the brain processing information beneath the level of conscious awareness. Research into implicit learning and heuristics—mental shortcuts based on previous experience—suggests that people can "sense" potential future events by drawing on hidden patterns and associations that they may not explicitly recognize.

In the case of Tatsuki's visions, it is possible that her subconscious mind was processing subtle signals from the environment—such as socio-political instability, environmental patterns, or emotional climates—without her consciously realizing it. Her dreams may have reflected this subconscious awareness, which she then interpreted as prophetic insight. As humans often rely on intuitive judgment to make decisions, this process could explain why some people "predict" certain outcomes.

2. Pattern Recognition and Cognitive Bias

A significant part of the process is pattern recognition, which involves identifying recurring patterns in data. The human brain is wired to recognize patterns—whether in numbers, behaviors, or events—and this cognitive function is crucial in problem-solving and decision-making. Pattern recognition also underpins many scientific and non-scientific predictions alike.

One of the scientific explanations for prophetic predictions, therefore, lies in confirmation bias, a cognitive phenomenon where people interpret information in ways that support their pre-existing beliefs or expectations. In this case, a person like Tatsuki may have perceived patterns or anomalies in her dreams that aligned with real-world events. Because such patterns seem to correlate, it strengthens the belief in her foresight. This is a classic example of how people may create a link between cause and effect, especially when they look back and see connections that may have been non-obvious at the time.

Pattern recognition is a vital skill for human survival, as it helps individuals anticipate threats, find food, or navigate the environment. It is plausible that Tatsuki's prophetic works could be an outgrowth of her brain's heightened sensitivity to patterns in the world—an ability to sense subtle undercurrents of change in society, technology, or nature that might not be immediately evident to others.

Psychological Theories on the Human Capacity for Foresight

Various psychological theories seek to explain the human capacity for foresight, particularly in terms of how individuals sense, predict, or anticipate future events. These theories focus on the role of subconscious signals, cognitive biases, and predictive reasoning in shaping human experience.

1. Subconscious Signals and Predictive Reasoning

One well-established psychological theory is that of predictive coding, which suggests that the brain constantly makes predictions about the world and updates them as new information becomes available. This is an adaptive function—based on past experiences—that helps individuals navigate uncertainty and make sense of ambiguous situations. According to predictive coding theory, our brains constantly generate hypotheses about the future based on sensory input and prior knowledge. When an individual encounters new information, the brain compares it with these predictions, adjusting accordingly.

In terms of foresight, this means that when Tatsuki experiences a vision or premonition, her brain might be drawing on past patterns—emotional, environmental, or cultural—without her conscious awareness. She may be attuned to certain subtle cues or phenomena that signal the potential for future events. This aligns with the idea that we do not consciously "see" the future, but our brains may be able to anticipate it, using a framework of prediction that guides behavior.

2. The Role of Memory and Recollection

Another psychological theory that could explain Tatsuki's predictive visions is retroactive inference. This phenomenon involves the brain recalling and making sense of past events in ways that give the illusion of foresight. For example, when a disaster occurs that Tatsuki had earlier depicted in her work, her readers might begin to connect her past illustrations with present events. This leads to a retroactive belief that Tatsuki had "predicted" the event, even though the prediction may have been based on current and foreseeable trends or subtle cues that were not immediately recognized.

3. The Psychology of Superstition

Cognitive psychology also offers insights into how people may interpret and attribute meaning to intuitive or predictive experiences. Superstition and magical thinking can influence how individuals perceive premonitions. When people experience a vivid dream or premonition that later correlates with a real-world event, they often interpret it as a prophetic experience. This psychological phenomenon occurs because the brain tends to look for patterns and meaning, especially when faced with uncertainty. In the case of Tatsuki, her visions might be seen through this lens, where her predictions are interpreted as prophetic symbols, reinforcing the belief that she is seeing into the future.

A Comparison of Tatsuki's Visions with Scientifically-Based Methods of Forecasting Events (e.g., Seismology, Epidemiology)

While Tatsuki's visions operate in the realm of the subjective and intuitive, scientific forecasting relies on empirical data and mathematical models to predict future events. By examining the differences and similarities between her work and scientific methods, we can gain a deeper understanding of how prophecy and science intersect.

1. Seismology

Seismology, the scientific study of earthquakes, offers a direct comparison to Tatsuki's predictions of seismic events. Seismologists use data from sensors that measure ground movements to predict the likelihood of earthquakes, using models based on geological patterns and plate tectonics. While it is currently impossible to predict the exact time and location of an earthquake with precision, earthquake forecasting is based on probabilistic models that can identify areas at higher risk.

Tatsuki's prediction of the Tōhoku earthquake, for example, aligns with the broader scientific understanding of Japan's susceptibility to earthquakes. While Tatsuki may not have had access to the same data as seismologists, her vision of a future catastrophe could be seen as her intuitive response to the ongoing seismic risks in the region. In both cases, predictions are based on an understanding of patterns—whether they are geological or emotional.

2. Epidemiology

Epidemiology, the study of disease distribution and determinants, operates similarly to seismology but in the context of public health. Using data on disease outbreaks, transmission rates, and population vulnerabilities, epidemiologists predict the likelihood of future outbreaks. For example, the 2020 COVID-19 pandemic was predicted by some researchers based on past global health trends and the nature of viral diseases.

Tatsuki's prediction of the COVID-19 pandemic, though seemingly a product of her dreams, aligns with the scientific principles behind forecasting disease outbreaks. By tracking trends in zoonotic diseases and the likelihood of pandemics, health professionals can make predictions based on available data. Tatsuki's prediction might be seen as her intuitive recognition of global health risks, which, much like the science of epidemiology, relies on the observation of existing patterns—though hers were conceptual and based on personal insights rather than data analysis.

The science of prophetic predictions, particularly in the context of Ryo Tatsuki's work, highlights the complex interaction between intuition, pattern recognition, and subconscious processing. While prophetic visions cannot be scientifically quantified or predicted with certainty, understanding the psychological and neurological processes that underpin intuition and pre- diction helps to frame how such visions may emerge. Whether driven by the subconscious recognition of trends, environmental signals, or emotional undercurrents, Tatsuki's visions reflect a broader human tendency to sense and respond to the unknown. When compared to scientific methods, Tatsuki's work invites reflection on how both empirical research and intuitive insight can offer valuable perspectives on understanding future events.

Appendix D: Case Studies of Other Notable Prophecies

Detailed Accounts of Other Famous Prophetic Figures

Ryo Tatsuki's prophetic works draw comparisons to other famous figures whose predictions have made significant cultural impacts. These mystics and visionaries, including Baba Vanga, Nostradamus, and Edgar Cayce, are often cited for their ability to foresee future events, some of which were later interpreted as eerily accurate. While the nature of their visions varies, the enduring fascination with these figures speaks to the universal human desire to understand and predict the future. Below are detailed accounts of each of these figures.

1. Baba Vanga

- Full Name: Vangelia Pandeva Dimitrova (1911–1996)
- Region: Bulgaria
- Known For: Clairvoyance, predicting major world events

Background: Baba Vanga, often referred to as the "Nostradamus of the Balkans," was a blind mystic who became famous for her predictions about the future. Born in 1911, she lost her sight at a young age and reportedly began experiencing visions and receiving messages from spirits. Over the course of her life, she made many predictions about political events, natural disasters, and other global occurrences.

Notable Predictions:

- The breakup of the Soviet Union.
- The 9/11 terrorist attacks.
- The rise of ISIS and the European refugee crisis.
- Predictions about natural disasters, including earthquakes and floods.

Interpretation and Reception: Baba Vanga's predictions are often vague and open to interpretation. Some of her followers claim that her visions were not only accurate but were communicated to her through divine or spiritual means. However, many of her predictions were generalized or framed in ways that could apply to multiple events, leading critics to dismiss them as post-hoc interpretations. Her influence, however, remains significant in certain parts of the world, where she is revered as a prophet.

2. Nostradamus

- Full Name: Michel de Nostredame (1503–1566)
- Region: France
- Known For: Prophecies written in quatrains

Background: Nostradamus was a French astrologer, physician, and seer best known for his book Les Prophéties, a collection of 942 poetic quatrains that are said to predict future events. Nostradamus's predictions span a wide range of topics, from natural disasters to the rise of political figures and the fate of nations. His work has been interpreted as a significant influence on the understanding of prophetic art.

Notable Predictions:

- The rise of Adolf Hitler.
- The French Revolution.
- The Great Fire of London in 1666.
- The September 11 attacks.

Interpretation and Reception: Nostradamus's prophecies are famous for their cryptic and vague language. His quatrains are often considered to be highly metaphorical, which allows for multiple interpretations. Throughout history, readers have reinterpreted his works to fit contemporary events. Many see Nostradamus as a mystic whose visions were tied to astrological insights, while others regard his work as a collection of general predictions with little to no specific relevance to actual events. Despite this, his popularity as a prophetic figure remains, and his works continue to inspire both believers and skeptics.

3. Edgar Cayce

- Full Name: Edgar Cayce (1877–1945)
- Region: United States
- Known For: Psychic readings, predictions on health, politics, and spiritual matters

Background: Edgar Cayce was an American psychic known as the "Sleeping Prophet." He gave thousands of readings, many while in a trance state, offering predictions about future events, guidance on health, and insights into spiritual matters. Unlike Nostradamus and Baba Vanga, Cayce's work was deeply intertwined with medical advice, and he is particularly known for his holistic approach to healing.

Notable Predictions:

- The Great Depression.
- World War II and its political aftermath.
- Predictions of a rise in global consciousness and the need for spiritual renewal.
- Earth changes, including a shift in the Earth's poles and catastrophic events.

Interpretation and Reception: Cayce's predictions were diverse, ranging from the political to the spiritual. His followers viewed his trance-based readings as a form of divine guidance, especially regarding healing and spirituality. He gained a significant following during his lifetime and his legacy endures, particularly through the Edgar Cayce Foundation, which continues to promote his teachings. Critics, however, argue that many of his predictions were vague or drawn from a combination of common knowledge and intuitive reasoning.

Analysis of How Their Predictions Were Received and Interpreted Across Time and Culture

The predictions made by Baba Vanga, Nostradamus, and Edgar Cayce were received with varying degrees of belief and skepticism, depending on the time period, cultural context, and the personal beliefs of the audience. These figures, though widely known and respected by their followers, have also faced significant criticism from those who argue that their predictions were simply general statements that could apply to many events.

1. Cultural Reception:

Baba Vanga enjoyed particular reverence in the Balkans and parts of Eastern Europe, where she was viewed as a mystic with supernatural abilities. Her predictions, often involving global politics and natural disasters, were viewed as evidence of her clairvoyant power. In contrast, Western audiences have been more skeptical of her abilities, often viewing her predictions as coincidental or based on ambiguous language.

Nostradamus' influence spanned Europe and later the globe, particularly in the 20th century. His cryptic quatrains have been interpreted by countless scholars, journalists, and conspiracy theorists, often reshaped to fit contemporary events. Nostradamus's work remains a cornerstone in the study of prophetic art, with adherents and skeptics alike continuing to argue over the significance of his predictions.

Edgar Cayce's readings had a profound impact in the United States, particularly in the realms of alternative medicine and spirituality. His work has influenced countless holistic healers, New Age practitioners, and people seeking spiritual enlightenment. His ability to predict geopolitical events, however, was viewed with a mix of curiosity and skepticism, particularly among those who viewed his predictions as divinely inspired.

2. Interpretation of Predictions:

Predictions made by all three figures were often vague or open-ended, leaving them open to reinterpretation. Critics have often noted that the more general the prophecy, the easier it is to align it with actual events after they occur. This is one reason why prophetic figures like Baba Vanga, Nostradamus, and Edgar Cayce remain controversial—many of their predictions seem to be crafted in ways that can be applied to various situations, giving rise to a confirmation bias.

Supporters argue that these figures were ahead of their time and able to tap into insights that modern science or conventional wisdom could not yet predict. Whether through spiritual insight, astrological knowledge, or intuitive prowess, these figures' works have remained a part of cultural discussions, especially when their predictions align with major world events.

Comparison of Tatsuki's Prophecies to Those of Other Mystics and Visionaries

When comparing Ryo Tatsuki's prophecies to those of other well-known visionaries like Baba Vanga, Nostradamus, and Edgar Cayce, several key differences and similarities emerge.

1. Prediction Accuracy and Specificity:

Tatsuki's prophecies, much like Nostradamus's, were often tied to specific, real-world events—such as the Tōhoku earthquake or the COVID-19 pandemic—which have since been validated. Her ability to predict specific disasters brings a certain level of credibility to her work, though like Baba Vanga's and Nostradamus's, her predictions were often generalized and left open to various interpretations.

Baba Vanga and Nostradamus both made predictions that were frequently vague, allowing them to be applied retroactively to major world events. This characteristic aligns more closely with the prophetic style seen in Edgar Cayce's predictions, where his readings could be interpreted in multiple ways.

Tatsuki's work, by contrast, is more rooted in personal experience and intuitive insight, rather than claims of divine or astrological knowledge. Her artwork and dreams create a narrative that merges intuition with emotional storytelling, making her prophecies less abstract than those of other mystics.

2. Art as a Medium for Prophecy:

Tatsuki's use of manga as the medium for her prophecies distinguishes her from figures like Baba Vanga, Nostradamus, and Cayce, who communicated their visions through oral readings, written quatrains, or trance states. Manga, as a visual storytelling medium, allows for a more visceral, emotional connection to the future, which is a significant departure from the text-based prophecies of the other figures.

Like Nostradamus, who used cryptic verses to convey his predictions,

Tatsuki employs symbols and emotions to communicate her visions. However, Tatsuki's art is more intuitive and personal, while the others relied on more formalized prophetic language or trance-like states.

3. Cultural Context and Reception:

While Baba Vanga and Nostradamus are primarily seen as figures of historical and spiritual prophecy, Tatsuki's work aligns more with the contemporary, secular world of manga and graphic novels, blending art with foresight. The reception of Tatsuki's work has been more global, gaining a following not just in Japan but worldwide, especially within the manga and anime communities.

While Ryo Tatsuki's work shares similarities with prophetic figures like Baba Vanga, Nostradamus, and Edgar Cayce, it also stands apart due to its unique medium of manga and its focus on personal intuition and emotional resonance. Her visions, though rooted in the same human need to predict and understand the future, are presented in a way that combines artistic expression with prophetic insight, offering readers both a narrative and a reflection on the emotional and psychological effects of facing the unknown.

Appendix E: Understanding the Tōhoku Earthquake and Tsunami

A Timeline of Events Surrounding the 2011 Disaster

The Tōhoku earthquake and subsequent tsunami of March 11, 2011, was one of the most catastrophic natural disasters in modern history, causing widespread devastation across northeastern Japan. The earthquake and tsunami not only resulted in significant loss of life but also triggered a nuclear crisis at the Fukushima Daiichi Nuclear Power Plant. Below is a timeline of key events surrounding the disaster:

March 11, 2011 – 2:46 PM (Japan Standard Time): A massive undersea earthquake, measuring 9.0 magnitude, struck off the coast of northeastern Japan, approximately 130 kilometers (81 miles) east of the Tōhoku region. It is the strongest earthquake ever recorded in Japan and one of the five strongest earthquakes in the world since modern seismography began.

2:47 PM – Aftershock and Immediate Effects: The initial earthquake lasted approximately 6 minutes, and the ground shaking was felt throughout Japan. The earthquake triggered a series of violent aftershocks, some of which reached magnitudes of 7.0 or higher. The shockwaves were so powerful that they were felt as far away as China and the Philippines.

2:49 PM – Tsunami Warning Issued: Following the earthquake, a tsunami warning was immediately issued by the Japan Meteorological Agency. The initial tsunami waves were expected to reach up to 10 meters (33 feet) in height along the coast.

2:50 PM – Tsunami Waves Hit the Coast: Within minutes of the earthquake, tsunami waves began to hit the northeastern coastline of Japan, including the cities of Sendai, Ishinomaki, and Minamisanriku. The waves reached a height of up to 40 meters (130 feet) in some areas, inundating entire towns and villages.

4:00 PM – Fukushima Daiichi Nuclear Disaster: The earthquake and tsunami caused severe damage to the Fukushima Daiichi Nuclear Power Plant. The facility's reactors lost power, triggering a failure of the cooling systems and leading to the release of radioactive material. The situation quickly escalated into a nuclear crisis, with multiple explosions and the evacuation of nearby areas.

March 12, 2011 – Rescue and Relief Operations Begin: Emergency response teams, including the Japan Self-Defense Forces (JSDF), as well as international teams, were mobilized to assist in search and rescue operations. The extent of the damage made it difficult to reach affected areas, and many cities were left without power, water, or transportation.

March 14, 2011 – Fukushima Nuclear Plant Crisis Escalates: As the Fukushima Daiichi Nuclear Power Plant continued to suffer from explosions and radiation leaks, a Level 7 nuclear accident was declared, marking the highest level of nuclear disaster on the International Nuclear Event Scale (INES). Tens of thousands of people were evacuated from the surrounding 30-kilometer radius.

March 11, 2012 – One-Year Anniversary: A nationwide memorial service was held to remember the more than 15,000 people who lost their lives in the disaster. Many people still remained displaced due to ongoing radiation concerns and the extensive damage to infrastructure.

A Technical Overview of the Geological and Environmental Factors Leading to the Event

The 2011 Tōhoku earthquake and tsunami were the result of complex geological and environmental factors, primarily involving the movement of tectonic plates beneath the Earth's surface.

1. The Japan Trench and Subduction Zones

The earthquake occurred along the Japan Trench, a subduction zone where the Pacific Plate is being forced beneath the North American Plate. This tectonic boundary is one of the most active and dangerous in the world, and it is responsible for the frequent occurrence of earthquakes and tsunamis along Japan's eastern coastline.

The Pacific Plate is moving westward and is pushed beneath the continental North American Plate at a rate of about 8-9 cm (3-4 inches) per year. As the plates interact, they accumulate immense stress. Eventually, this stress is released in the form of a powerful earthquake, a process known as subduction zone megathrust earthquakes.

2. The Earthquake

The Tōhoku earthquake, known as the Great East Japan Earthquake, was the result of a megathrust event, meaning that it was caused by a sudden rupture along the subduction zone. This rupture occurred over an area of about 500 kilometers (310 miles) along the fault line. The earthquake released an enormous amount of energy—equivalent to several thousand atomic bombs— and was felt across much of East Asia.

3. Tsunami Generation

The seismic activity caused by the earthquake lifted the sea floor along the subduction zone by several meters, displacing an enormous volume of water. This displacement triggered the tsunami that followed. Tsunamis are typically caused by undersea earthquakes, and the large-scale vertical movement of the ocean floor in this case was a key factor in the tsunami's destructive power.

The tsunami waves were not immediately noticeable in deep water, but as the waves approached the shallow coastal regions, their height increased dramatically. When they struck Japan's eastern coastline, the waves were amplified by the narrow bays and coastal topography, resulting in tsunami waves up to 40 meters high in some areas.

4. The Impact of Aftershocks

Following the main earthquake, Japan experienced numerous aftershocks, some of which were large enough to cause further damage and instability in already weakened buildings and infrastructure. The largest aftershock, a 7.9 magnitude quake, occurred just a few hours later, prolonging the crisis and hampering rescue efforts.

The Aftermath: How Japan Responded to the Catastrophe, Including Recovery and Rebuilding Efforts

In the aftermath of the Tōhoku earthquake and tsunami, Japan faced monumental challenges in terms of immediate rescue operations, recovery, and rebuilding. The response to the disaster was one of coordination on an unprecedented scale, with the government, local authorities, and international aid organizations working together to address the humanitarian crisis and the long-term rebuilding efforts.

1. Immediate Relief and Rescue Efforts

The Japanese government deployed the Japan Self-Defense Forces (JSDF), who provided search and rescue teams, distributed food and water, and assisted in medical care and shelter. Over 100,000 personnel were mobilized in the immediate aftermath of the disaster.

The international community, including countries like the United States, China, and South Korea, sent aid in the form of medical supplies, food, and search-and-rescue teams. The United Nations also provided support through its relief agencies.

Evacuations from the Fukushima area were particularly urgent, as the nuclear crisis at the Fukushima Daiichi Nuclear Power Plant threatened to spread radioactive contamination. Over 160,000 people were evacuated from the area surrounding the plant.

2. Infrastructure Damage and Rebuilding

The Tōhoku region suffered extensive damage to both infrastructure and housing. Thousands of buildings were destroyed or severely damaged by the tsunami, and transportation networks, including railways, airports, and highways, were incapacitated in many areas.

The Japanese government announced an emergency relief package worth billions of dollars to assist with reconstruction efforts, focusing on rebuilding homes, infrastructure, and public services. However, the challenges were immense, and it was estimated that the total cost of the disaster would exceed \$300 billion—making it one of the most expensive natural disasters in history.

3. Fukushima Nuclear Crisis and Response

The nuclear disaster at Fukushima became one of the most complex aspects of the aftermath. The Tokyo Electric Power Company (TEPCO) faced severe criticism for its handling of the crisis, and the Japanese government committed to a massive cleanup and decommissioning process. This ongoing process, expected to take several decades, involves the removal of radioactive fuel, the containment of contaminated water, and the management of nuclear waste.

The Fukushima disaster also led to widespread debate in Japan over the future of nuclear energy. In the years following the disaster, Japan gradually phased out its reliance on nuclear power and invested more heavily in renewable energy sources.

4. Long-Term Recovery and Psychological Impact

Beyond the physical reconstruction, Japan also faced the long-term psychological effects of the disaster. Thousands of people were displaced, and the trauma of losing loved ones, homes, and livelihoods was deeply felt. The mental health challenges faced by survivors, including post-traumatic stress disorder (PTSD) and anxiety, became a major focus in recovery efforts.

Communities that had been devastated by the tsunami began rebuilding their lives with a focus on resilience, unity, and rebuilding social bonds. While the recovery process was slow, Japan's commitment to rebuilding not only the infrastructure but also the community spirit of the affected areas became a symbol of the nation's strength.

5. Disaster Preparedness and Lessons Learned

In the years following the disaster, Japan has placed a significant emphasis on improving disaster preparedness, building more resilient infrastructure, and enhancing its early warning systems. The 2011 disaster underscored the importance of being prepared for multiple forms of catastrophe, and Japan's efforts in the aftermath have been regarded as a model for other countries vulnerable to natural disasters.

The 2011 Tōhoku earthquake and tsunami was a defining moment in Japan's history. It was an event of unparalleled devastation, but it also demonstrated Japan's resilience in the face of unimaginable loss. The disaster also highlighted the importance of global cooperation, disaster preparedness, and the ongoing efforts to understand and mitigate the impact of natural phenomena. The recovery and rebuilding process continues, and the lessons learned from this catastrophic event continue to shape how Japan—and the world—respond to future challenges.

Appendix F: The Impact of the COVID-19 Pandemic

A Global Timeline of the Pandemic's Onset, Spread, and Ongoing Effects

The COVID-19 pandemic, caused by the SARS-CoV-2 virus, has been one of the most significant global events of the 21st century, affecting nearly every aspect of daily life. Below is a detailed timeline of the pandemic's onset, its global spread, and the ongoing effects:

1. December 2019 – Initial Outbreak in Wuhan, China

December 8, 2019: The first reported cases of what would later be identified as COVID-19 appeared in Wuhan, China. At this stage, the illness was not yet fully understood, and the virus was initially thought to be a form of pneumonia.

December 31, 2019: China alerted the World Health Organization (WHO) about several cases of an unusual pneumonia in Wuhan, although the exact cause was still undetermined.

2. January 2020 – Early Spread and Global Awareness

January 7, 2020: Chinese authorities identified a new coronavirus as the cause of the pneumonia cases. The virus was temporarily named 2019-nCoV, later becoming known as SARS-CoV-2.

January 13, 2020: The first confirmed case outside China was reported in Thailand, marking the beginning of the global spread.

January 30, 2020: The WHO declared the COVID-19 outbreak a public health emergency of international concern (PHEIC), although the virus had not yet become a pandemic.

3. February 2020 – Spread Across Continents

February 2020: Cases continued to spread rapidly across the globe, with countries like Italy, South Korea, and Iran seeing significant outbreaks. International travel restrictions were implemented, and public health systems began to struggle with the rapidly increasing number of infections.

February 28, 2020: The United States reported its first COVID-19-related death in Washington state, marking the beginning of widespread concern in North America.

4. March 2020 – WHO Declares a Global Pandemic

March 11, 2020: The World Health Organization declared COVID-19 a global pandemic, recognizing that the virus had spread to nearly every country in the world.

March 2020: Many countries, including Italy, Spain, France, and the United States, imposed widespread lockdowns, closing businesses, schools, and public spaces in an attempt to curb the virus' spread.

5. April 2020 – Peak of Initial Wave in Many Countries

April 2020: In many countries, including Italy and Spain, hospitals became overwhelmed with COVID-19 patients. The pandemic put immense strain on global healthcare systems. The U.S. became one of the hardest-hit countries, with large cities like New York becoming epicenters of the crisis.

April 2020: Governments enacted emergency measures, including economic stimulus packages, to support businesses and citizens affected by the pandemic.

6. July 2020 – The First Wave in Some Regions Begins to Subside

July 2020: Many countries that had imposed strict lockdown measures saw some success in reducing case numbers, but the virus continued to spread in regions with weaker healthcare systems, particularly in parts of Africa, South America, and Southeast Asia.

7. November 2020 – Vaccine Development and Approval

November 2020: Several pharmaceutical companies, including Pfizer and Moderna, announced that their COVID-19 vaccines had demonstrated high efficacy in clinical trials.

December 2020: The U.S. Food and Drug Administration (FDA) and the European Medicines Agency (EMA) approved the first COVID-19 vaccines for emergency use, marking the beginning of global vaccination efforts.

8. 2021 – Vaccination Rollout and Variants

January 2021: The vaccination campaign began in countries like the United States, United Kingdom, and Israel, with health workers and vulnerable populations being prioritized.

February 2021:Variants of concern began emerging, including the Alpha variant (first identified in the UK) and later the Delta and Omicron variants, which were more transmissible and caused renewed surges in cases.

August 2021: Vaccination campaigns expanded globally, although vaccine access remained a challenge in many low-income countries.

9. 2022 – Ongoing Challenges and Global Impact

2022: As vaccination rates increased, many countries began to ease restrictions, but the pandemic continued to affect global life. Ongoing waves of infections, particularly from variants like Omicron, delayed full recovery. Governments focused on adjusting their strategies for living with COVID-19, balancing public health measures with the need to resume economic and social activities.

10. 2023 and Beyond – Long-Term Effects

By 2023, many parts of the world were moving toward a state of living with COVID-19, with countries adopting more sustainable approaches to public health and vaccination. However, the global mental health crisis, economic recovery, and vaccine equity remained ongoing challenges. Some regions continue to face outbreaks and surges, requiring continuous adaptation of health policies.

How the Virus Shaped Public Health Policy, Economies, and Daily Life Worldwide

The COVID-19 pandemic has had a profound effect on public health policy, economies, and the daily lives of people worldwide.

1. Public Health Policy

Global Health Systems: The pandemic tested healthcare systems around the world, with many countries facing severe shortages in medical supplies, healthcare workers, and hospital beds. The crisis prompted massive invest- ments in public health infrastructure, including increased funding for research and rapid vaccine development.

Quarantine and Isolation Measures: To contain the virus, governments implemented social distancing, lockdowns, and mandatory quarantine mea- sures. Public health agencies such as the CDC, WHO, and national governments issued guidance on mask-wearing, hand hygiene, and vaccination.

Health Disparities: The pandemic highlighted significant health disparities across socioeconomic groups and between countries. Vulnerable populations, including low-income communities and racial minorities, were dispropor- tionately affected by COVID-19, leading to calls for more equitable healthcare systems.

2. Economic Impact

Global Recession: The pandemic led to the global economic downturn, with many countries experiencing recession due to lockdowns, disrupted supply chains, and business closures. Unemployment rates surged, and millions of people were pushed into poverty.

Government Stimulus: In response, many governments implemented stimulus packages, unemployment benefits, and direct financial support to businesses and individuals. The U.S. CARES Act and similar programs in other countries provided relief to millions, although the long-term economic impact remains significant.

Shift to Remote Work: The pandemic accelerated the remote work trend, with many businesses adopting flexible work-from-home policies. This shift has led to long-term changes in how businesses operate, impacting real estate, commuting patterns, and office culture.

3. Social and Daily Life

Social Distancing and Mental Health: Social distancing measures led to widespread isolation and disruption of normal daily activities. Schools and universities closed, moving to online education, while restaurants, entertainment venues, and travel were restricted or shut down.

Psychological Impact: The pandemic caused a global mental health crisis, with increased rates of anxiety, depression, and PTSD. Concerns about job loss, health risks, and uncertainty about the future contributed to a rise in mental health issues worldwide. Governments and healthcare providers have worked to address this through mental health initiatives, though the effects remain long-lasting.

Changes in Consumer Behavior: The pandemic transformed consumer habits, with increased reliance on e-commerce, digital services, and con-tactless payments. People began spending more time online, leading to shifts in retail, entertainment, and media consumption.

The Societal Implications of the Pandemic and the Global Mental Health Crisis

The COVID-19 pandemic not only caused immediate health and economic damage but also brought lasting changes to society, with profound psychoso-cial and cultural implications.

1. Global Mental Health Crisis

The psychological toll of the pandemic has been one of its most far-reaching consequences. Lockdowns, social distancing, economic uncertainty, and the fear of contracting the virus led to a global mental health crisis. According to the World Health Organization (WHO), mental health conditions, including anxiety and depression, skyrocketed, particularly among vulnerable populations.

The pandemic also led to increased stress for frontline workers, healthcare professionals, and caregivers, many of whom faced burnout due to extended hours and the emotional strain of caring for patients in overwhelmed health-care systems.

2. Education and Child Development

The closure of schools and the shift to remote learning created significant disruptions for students, especially for those in under-resourced communities. The loss of social interactions, extracurricular activities, and in-person learning has had long-term implications for children's social development and academic progress.

The shift to digital education also highlighted the digital divide, with many students lacking access to necessary technology or reliable internet connections.

3. The Future of Global Health and Preparedness

The COVID-19 pandemic has brought global health inequalities to the forefront, and post-pandemic, there is an increasing push for better health equity, greater international collaboration, and preparedness for future pandemics. The crisis has also underscored the importance of investing in global health systems, research, and pandemic preparedness.

The COVID-19 pandemic has reshaped the world in ways that will continue to reverberate across all aspects of life—public health, economies, mental health, and societal norms. While the immediate crisis may subside as vaccination efforts progress and economies recover, the long-term effects of the pandemic on mental health, global health systems, and social behavior will persist. It has forced societies worldwide to confront vulnerabilities, reassess public health strategies, and acknowledge the importance of resilience in the face of uncertainty.

Appendix G: Prophetic Predictions and Their Cultural Impact

Exploration of How Prophetic Works, Including Tatsuki's, Have Influenced Cultural Narratives and Public Perceptions

Prophetic works have always played a significant role in shaping cultural narratives and public perceptions, both through their direct impact on society and through their reflective nature in art, literature, and media. Prophecies, whether viewed as true visions of the future or as allegories of human experience, tap into the universal human desire to understand the unknown and prepare for the future.

1. Tatsuki's Influence on Cultural Narratives

Ryo Tatsuki's prophetic visions, particularly through her manga, have contributed to the broader cultural conversation about fate, resilience, and the unpredictability of life. Her work often portrays characters navigating catastrophic events, reflecting the emotional and psychological consequences of disasters. This resonates deeply with global audiences living in an era marked by environmental crises, political instability, and technological change.

Tatsuki's ability to combine intuitive artistry with predictive storytelling has created a narrative space where people can confront their fears and uncertainties. Her works are not just predictions but reflections of human vulnerability and resilience. By projecting future disasters and showing how her characters respond, she encourages readers to reflect on their own ability to withstand crises.

As her prophecies came true in the form of the 2011 Tōhoku earthquake, the COVID-19 pandemic, and other global events, her work has gained increasing attention. Tatsuki's growing global recognition reflects how prophecy—whether through dreams, art, or mysticism—continues to capture the imagination of society, serving both as a warning and a source of reflection.

2. Prophecy and Public Perception

The portrayal of prophetic figures and their predictions shapes public perceptions of uncertainty and control over the future. Tatsuki's work, as well as that of other visionaries, makes people question the nature of fate— whether events are preordained or the result of collective action. Prophetic predictions, especially those that come to pass, can influence how people prepare for the future, often instilling fear or a sense of inevitability.

In societies facing existential challenges, such as climate change, political in-stability, and public health crises, the role of prophecy in providing cautionary tales or visions of hope becomes especially significant. Prophetic narratives can inspire action, whether through disaster preparedness, spiritual reflection, or social change.

How Prophecy is Portrayed in Media, Literature, and Popular Culture

The influence of prophecy extends far beyond Tatsuki's work, permeating media, literature, and popular culture. Prophecies have become central themes in stories about human struggle, societal collapse, and the search for meaning in times of crisis.

1. Media and Pop Culture

Film and Television: Prophetic themes have been prevalent in cinematic storytelling, with films like The Matrix, The Terminator, and Children of

Men focusing on visions of dystopian futures, apocalyptic events, and the survival of humanity. These stories often involve characters who grapple with knowledge of the future or are caught in the cycle of predetermined events. The portrayal of prophetic figures in these films is a direct reflection of society's concerns about the future and its uncertain trajectory.

Television shows like The 100, The Walking Dead, and The Leftovers explore how societies cope with catastrophic events that have been foreseen or alluded to, often questioning whether humanity can change its fate. These shows mirror the real-world anxiety people feel about large-scale societal collapse or environmental disaster, providing an emotional outlet for viewers to engage with these anxieties.

The global popularity of apocalyptic themes in media, from superhero stories to speculative fiction, speaks to a societal preoccupation with future uncertainty, global crises, and existential questions. These narratives often ask whether individuals or societies can rewrite their futures in the face of impending disaster.

2. Literature

Prophecy has long been a central theme in literature, particularly in genres like dystopian fiction, science fiction, and fantasy. Authors like George Orwell (1984), Aldous Huxley (Brave New World), and Margaret Atwood (The Handmaid's Tale) used prophetic visions of the future to explore the consequences of unchecked power, technological overreach, and social inequality. These works tap into the desire to understand and predict the future in a way that forces readers to confront uncomfortable truths about society.

Fantasy novels, such as J.R.R. Tolkien's The Lord of the Rings or George R.R. Martin's A Song of Ice and Fire series, feature prophecies that drive the plots and character development, exploring themes of fate, destiny, and the struggle for control. These literary traditions have deep cultural roots, echoing classical works like the Greek tragedies, where prophecies often set the stage for conflict, heroism, and tragedy.

Prophetic literature, whether it comes in the form of novels, poetry, or plays, often uses the medium to express a cultural anxiety about the future—whether that future is dystopian, utopian, or apocalyptic. By presenting a speculative future, these stories invite readers to reflect on their current actions and choices, emphasizing that the future is not inevitable but shaped by collective decisions.

3. Popular Culture and Prophetic Archetypes

The archetype of the prophet or seer has been a constant in popular culture. In modern times, these figures have evolved from religious prophets to more secular, mystical, or psychic figures. Popular media has embraced characters like psychic detectives, fortune tellers, and time travelers, who often serve as catalysts for the narrative. These characters may predict future events, serve as guides for protagonists, or warn of impending disasters, often reflecting societal anxieties or hopes about the future.

Psychic and clairvoyant figures in popular culture are often presented as individuals with a deep connection to the future, providing insight that others cannot perceive. This portrayal influences the public's view of prophetic ability, shaping how people see figures like Tatsuki. Though the medium may differ, the underlying narrative remains consistent: the future is something that can be known, understood, and, sometimes, changed.

The Societal Impact of Prophetic Beliefs, Both Positive and Negative

Prophetic beliefs have a profound impact on society, influencing everything from policy decisions and public behavior to individual and collective psychology. The societal impact of prophecy can be both positive and negative, depending on how the belief system is integrated into the broader social fabric.

1. Positive Impact

Hope and Resilience: In times of crisis, prophetic narratives can provide a sense of hope and clarity, offering individuals a way to make sense of chaos and uncertainty. For example, prophetic works that focus on resilience in the face of catastrophe can inspire people to take proactive steps to prepare for or prevent future disasters. Tatsuki's work, for instance, focuses on the human capacity to endure, survive, and rebuild in the aftermath of disaster, a message that resonates deeply with readers in a world defined by uncertainty.

Motivation for Change: Prophecies that predict an inevitable crisis can also motivate individuals and societies to take preventative action. This has been observed throughout history, where the belief in an impending disaster—whether due to war, disease, or environmental collapse—has sparked social movements, innovations in technology, or policy reforms aimed at addressing the perceived threat. Prophetic works that call for positive social change can serve as a catalyst for collective action.

Spiritual and Existential Reflection: Prophecies, especially those with spiritual or philosophical dimensions, can prompt individuals to reflect on their lives, actions, and the broader meaning of existence. They can encourage self-improvement, a reevaluation of priorities, or a deeper connection to spiritual or philosophical beliefs.

2. Negative Impact

Fear and Paranoia: Prophecies, especially those that predict catastrophic events, can generate fear and paranoia. The anticipation of an inevitable disaster can lead to anxiety, social unrest, and panic. In extreme cases, belief in prophecies has led to mass hysteria, apocalyptic movements, or violent actions by groups convinced that the future they've foreseen is unavoidable.

Determinism and Fatalism: Prophetic beliefs can sometimes encourage a fatalistic or deterministic worldview, in which individuals feel powerless to change the future. If people believe that an event is predestined, they may become passive, resigning themselves to fate rather than taking action to improve their lives or prevent harm.

Exploitation: Throughout history, various individuals and groups have exploited prophetic beliefs for personal gain or political control. Religious or political leaders may use prophecy to manipulate populations, gaining power or support by convincing people that they hold the key to salvation or survival. In this way, prophecy can be weaponized for control.

Prophetic works, including Tatsuki's, have had a profound influence on how societies engage with the future. Whether inspiring hope, caution, or action, these narratives provide insight into the universal human need to understand the unknown. Prophecies in media, literature, and popular culture reflect both our fears and our aspirations, while the societal impact of prophetic beliefs—both positive and negative—shapes our collective response to uncertainty. By examining the role of prophecy, we not only engage with visions of what might come but also explore how we, as individuals and societies, navigate an unpredictable world.

Appendix H: Ryo Tatsuki's Influence on Modern Manga and Graphic Novels

Analysis of Tatsuki's Influence on Contemporary Manga Artists and Writers

Ryo Tatsuki's work, particularly her prophetic approach to storytelling through manga, has had a lasting influence on contemporary manga artists and writers. While Tatsuki was initially recognized for her intuitive and emotional storytelling, her influence has since extended beyond the borders of her genre, impacting the development of both narrative styles and thematic exploration in manga.

1. Influence on Genre Evolution

Tatsuki's blending of art and prophecy has created a distinct genre within manga that merges the emotional depth of literary storytelling with the speculative and often apocalyptic themes of science fiction and supernatural fiction. Many modern manga artists have adopted aspects of Tatsuki's approach, particularly in the way she integrates personal visions and collective societal fears into larger narrative frameworks.

Psychological Depth and Emotion: Contemporary manga artists, such as Junji Ito and Naoki Urasawa, have drawn inspiration from Tatsuki's ability to convey complex emotional landscapes. Her works, often centered around disaster, fear, and survival, resonate with artists who seek to capture the psychological toll of global crises. Manga like Urasawa's 20th Century Boys or Ito's Uzumaki similarly blend personal and societal catastrophes with deep psychological exploration, a thematic element that Tatsuki pioneered.

Prophetic and Apocalyptic Themes: Tatsuki's incorporation of prophetic visions has influenced manga writers who deal with the end of the world, catastrophic events, or the consequences of unchecked human behavior. Hiroshi Sakurazaka's All You Need Is Kill and Masashi Kishimoto's Naruto incorporate apocalyptic or end-of-the-world themes, often with a focus on human perseverance in the face of overwhelming odds. Tatsuki's work paved the way for these types of narratives by creating a genre that explores not only physical destruction but also the emotional, psychological, and social repercussions of disaster.

2. Interdisciplinary Influence: Tatsuki's impact extends beyond traditional manga artists to influence other creative fields, including graphic novels, animation, and even video game storytelling. Her ability to merge complex social commentary with visual art has inspired visual storytellers across the globe. The manga-style storytelling she championed can be seen in modern graphic novels, where complex emotional journeys are paired with speculative futures, dystopian worlds, or catastrophic events.

How Her Prophetic Approach to Storytelling Has Inspired New Genres and Thematic Explorations in Manga

Ryo Tatsuki's prophetic approach to storytelling—intertwining intuitive dreams with narrative fiction—has inspired a new generation of manga writers to explore futuristic and dystopian themes through a more personal and emotionally driven lens.

1. Emergence of the "Prophetic Manga" Genre

Tatsuki's integration of prophecy into the manga medium created a sub-genre that focuses on future predictions, visions, and intuitive insights. These elements bring the genre closer to both psychological thriller and supernatural drama, blurring the lines between realism and speculative fiction. Writers inspired by Tatsuki are now exploring themes of fate, resilience, and the unpredictability of life through their characters' psychic abilities or visions of future events.

Manga like Katsuhiro Otomo's Akira and \\Yū Koyama's Silence" combine prophetic visions with futuristic dystopias, focusing on how characters struggle against or embrace foreseen events. These works resonate with Tatsuki's influence by portraying societies facing the emotional and social impacts of a predicted collapse or disaster, while also questioning whether such fate can be changed.

The psychic detective genre also gained popularity due to Tatsuki's blending of prophecy and mystery. Contemporary manga such as Saki Hiwatari's Please Save My Earth blends psychic ability and disaster themes, with characters experiencing past-life visions that shape their current fates. In this, Tatsuki's approach to emotional storytelling—rooted in personal and societal reflections on foreseen futures—has allowed other writers to develop deeply complex narratives.

2. Exploration of Social and Cultural Themes

Tatsuki's works often explored the psychological toll of future catastrophes, a narrative focus that has deeply influenced modern manga. Artists and writers have begun to embrace stories that don't just focus on action or spectacle, but on the human experience in the face of inevitable, or perceived inevitable, destruction.

Humanity's Struggle for Survival: Much like Tatsuki's characters, those in Satoshi Kon's Tokyo Godfathers or Paprika are often forced to confront personal trauma and the looming sense of catastrophe. This style of introspective storytelling has become more common in manga, where protagonists do not simply react to external events but question their own beliefs, desires, and responsibilities in the face of a larger societal or existential crisis.

Social Commentary through Prophecy: Tatsuki's prophetic work often focused on the emotional and psychological effects of disaster, highlighting the societal need for connection and resilience in times of crisis. Takeshi Obata and Tsugumi Ohba's Death Note, which tackles moral and existential questions, also reflects these themes, focusing on characters who see themselves as part of a larger, fate-driven narrative.

A Look at How Her Work Has Impacted Global Readership, Particularly Among Young Adults

Ryo Tatsuki's work has had a significant impact on global readership, particularly among young adults. Her ability to combine relatable, emotional stories with futuristic and catastrophic events has resonated deeply with this demographic, who often face their own fears about the future, both on a personal level and as a part of a broader society.

1. Appeal to a Generation Facing Uncertainty

Tatsuki's work has found a particularly strong audience among young adults who are grappling with the challenges of a rapidly changing world. In an age where political unrest, environmental disaster, and global health crises often dominate the news cycle, Tatsuki's prophetic tales about disasters and societal collapse strike a chord with readers who are concerned about the future.

Tatsuki's themes of resilience, hope, and individual responsibility resonate with young readers, many of whom are navigating their own personal crises and fears about the state of the world. Manga readers, particularly in the millennial and Gen Z age groups, have found solace in Tatsuki's emotionally charged narratives, which combine the universal struggle for survival with a deeper psychological and emotional exploration of the human condition.

2. Global Influence through Manga and Anime

The international success of manga and anime has made Tatsuki's work accessible to a global audience, influencing not only Japanese readers but also fans from countries around the world. Manga, often seen as a means to explore deeply personal and societal issues, has grown in popularity due to the emotional complexity of the characters and themes. Tatsuki's influence is felt in the broader manga and anime subculture, where storytelling is no longer just about entertainment, but also about social engagement and personal reflection.

Tatsuki's influence is particularly strong among young adult audiences, many of whom consume manga not just for escapism but for insight into their own fears, desires, and uncertainties. Young readers from countries such as the United States, Brazil, and France, where manga culture has flourished, have adopted Tatsuki's themes of prophecy, survival, and emotional resilience as part of their global cultural identity.

3. Adaptations and International Exposure

Tatsuki's work has been adapted into various forms of media, including anime, graphic novels, and interactive storytelling platforms, allowing her stories to reach an even wider audience. The growing acceptance of manga as a legitimate literary and artistic medium, particularly in the global young adult market, has ensured that Tatsuki's influence will continue to shape future generations of creators, writers, and artists.

Ryo Tatsuki's prophetic approach to storytelling has had a profound and lasting impact on the world of modern manga and graphic novels. Her blending of emotional, personal narratives with speculative and apocalyptic themes has created a genre that not only reflects global anxieties but also resonates deeply with young adults navigating an uncertain future. Tatsuki's influence can be seen in the thematic depth and psychological complexity of contemporary manga, as well as in the way it engages with global audiences. As her legacy continues to evolve, Tatsuki's work will undoubtedly inspire future generations of creators who seek to explore the human experience in the face of an unpredictable world.

Appendix I: Japan's Seismic Activity and Disaster Preparedness

Overview of Japan's Geographic Vulnerability to Earthquakes, Tsunamis, and Other Natural Disasters

Japan's geographic location places it at the intersection of several tectonic plates, making it one of the most seismically active regions in the world. The country's vulnerability to natural disasters, including earthquakes, tsunamis, typhoons, and volcanic eruptions, has shaped its history, culture, and disaster preparedness strategies.

1. Tectonic Plate Boundaries

Japan is located on the Pacific Ring of Fire, an area where several major tectonic plates meet, including the Pacific Plate, Philippine Sea Plate, Eurasian Plate, and North American Plate. These plates are constantly shifting, causing frequent earthquakes and volcanic activity. The Japan Trench and the Nankai Trough are subduction zones where the Pacific Plate and Philippine Sea Plate are forced beneath the North American Plate and Eurasian Plate, leading to powerful earthquakes and tsunamis.

2. Earthquakes

Earthquakes are the most common and devastating natural disasters in Japan. The country experiences thousands of small tremors each year, with significant quakes occurring on average once every few decades. These quakes can cause massive destruction, particularly in densely populated urban areas.

3. Tsunamis

Tsunamis are often triggered by undersea earthquakes. When the seafloor is abruptly displaced by seismic activity, it generates large waves that travel across the ocean at high speeds. When these waves reach the coast, they can cause catastrophic flooding and destruction. Tsunamis have historically been one of the most deadly natural disasters in Japan, especially in coastal cities.

4. Other Natural Disasters

In addition to earthquakes and tsunamis, Japan also faces threats from typhoons (tropical cyclones), volcanic eruptions, and landslides. Typhoons frequently make landfall in Japan, bringing heavy rain, strong winds, and the potential for flooding. Japan also has more than 100 active volcanoes, many of which pose a risk to nearby populations.

The History of Seismic Activity in Japan, with a Focus on Major Events

Japan's long history with seismic activity has led to an evolving approach to disaster preparedness. Below are some of the most significant seismic events in Japan's history:

1. The 1995 Kobe Earthquake (Great Hanshin Earthquake)

Date: January 17, 1995

Magnitude: 7.2

Location: Near the city of Kobe, Hyōgo Prefecture

Impact: The Kobe earthquake was one of Japan's deadliest earthquakes in modern history, claiming over 6,000 lives and causing widespread damage. The earthquake struck during the early morning hours, causing buildings to collapse, fires to break out, and transportation systems to fail. The earthquake's epicenter was located along the Nojima Fault near the densely populated Kansai region, affecting Kobe, Osaka, and surrounding areas.

Aftermath and Lessons Learned: The Kobe earthquake revealed significant weaknesses in Japan's disaster preparedness and emergency response systems. The destruction of buildings and infrastructure exposed the need for better earthquake-resistant construction standards. In the years that followed, Japan's focus shifted toward improving its disaster response and resilience strategies.

2. The 2011 Tōhoku Earthquake and Tsunami (Great East Japan Earthquake)

Date: March 11, 2011

Magnitude: 9.0

Location: Off the northeastern coast of Japan (Tōhoku region)

Impact: The Tōhoku earthquake was the strongest earthquake ever recorded in Japan and the fourth strongest in the world. The earthquake triggered a massive tsunami, with waves reaching heights of over 40 meters (131 feet) in some areas. The tsunami inundated large coastal areas, including Sendai and Ishinomaki, causing widespread destruction, the loss of more than 15,000 lives, and tens of thousands of people displaced. The tsunami also caused a nuclear disaster at the Fukushima Daiichi Nuclear Power Plant, which led to radioactive contamination and the evacuation of over 100,000 people.

Aftermath and Long-Term Effects: The Tōhoku disaster prompted Japan to rethink its approach to disaster preparedness. Despite having one of the most advanced earthquake early warning systems in the world, the scale of the tsunami's impact and the nuclear crisis raised questions about the effectiveness of preparedness measures in the face of such large-scale events. The disaster also led to a re-evaluation of Japan's nuclear energy policies, with many reactors being decommissioned or shut down for safety reasons.

3. The 2016 Kumamoto Earthquake

Date: April 14–16, 2016

Magnitude: 7.0

Location: Kumamoto Prefecture, Kyushu Island

Impact: This earthquake caused extensive damage to the city of Kumamoto and surrounding areas. The earthquake led to the collapse of buildings, widespread landslides, and significant infrastructure damage. Fortunately, the damage was less severe than the 1995 Kobe earthquake and the 2011 Tōhoku disaster, but it still resulted in dozens of fatalities and tens of thousands of people displaced.

Aftermath and Response: The 2016 Kumamoto earthquake highlighted the vulnerability of older buildings and infrastructure in Japan's rural regions. The earthquake response involved extensive recovery and rebuilding efforts, which further emphasized the need for stronger disaster preparedness in both urban and rural areas.

An Examination of Japan's Disaster Preparedness Infrastructure

Japan has one of the most advanced disaster preparedness infrastructures in the world. Over the decades, the country has invested heavily in earthquake-resistant technologies, early warning systems, and public education to mitigate the impact of natural disasters.

1. Earthquake-Resistant Buildings

Japan's building codes are among the strictest in the world, with a focus on earthquake resistance. High-rise buildings, bridges, and infrastructure are designed to withstand seismic activity, with advanced seismic dampers and flexible frameworks that allow buildings to sway rather than collapse during an earthquake. After the 1995 Kobe earthquake, Japan made further improvements to construction standards, particularly for older buildings.

The 2011 Tōhoku earthquake demonstrated the effectiveness of earthquake-resistant design in urban areas. Despite the devastation caused by the tsunami, buildings in places like Tokyo and Osaka were largely unaffected by the earthquake's shaking, thanks to rigorous construction practices. However, rural and older structures continue to pose challenges for Japan's disaster resilience.

2. Earthquake Early Warning Systems

Japan's Earthquake Early Warning (EEW) system is one of the most advanced in the world. The system uses a network of seismic sensors placed throughout the country to detect the initial seismic waves (P-waves) of an earthquake. Once detected, the system sends alerts to individuals and infrastructure before the more damaging seismic waves (S-waves) arrive.

The Japan Meteorological Agency (JMA) operates the system, which provides seconds to a few minutes of warning before the shaking begins. This allows people to take protective actions, such as ducking and covering, and helps prevent injuries. The system has been credited with saving lives during many significant events, including the 2011 Tōhoku earthquake.

3. Tsunami Warning Systems

Along with earthquake early warnings, Japan has a robust tsunami warning system that relies on buoys in the ocean, seafloor sensors, and rapid data analysis to predict the arrival of tsunami waves. When a major undersea earthquake occurs, the system immediately calculates the potential tsunami size and alerts the public.

Following the 2011 Tōhoku disaster, Japan implemented improvements to its tsunami warning systems. The height and arrival time of tsunami waves are now more accurately predicted, and evacuation procedures have been streamlined in coastal areas.

4. Public Education and Preparedness Drills

Japan's emphasis on disaster education has played a crucial role in its preparedness efforts. Public education campaigns teach citizens how to respond to earthquakes, tsunamis, and other natural disasters. Schools, workplaces, and local governments regularly conduct disaster drills, including evacuation drills, earthquake drills, and first aid training.

Japan also places a strong emphasis on community resilience, with local organizations and volunteer groups trained to assist in the aftermath of disasters. In many areas, citizens are encouraged to participate in neighborhood disaster preparedness programs to ensure that people know how to respond in case of an emergency.

Japan's geographical vulnerability to natural disasters has shaped the country's disaster preparedness infrastructure, making it one of the most disaster-resilient nations in the world. From earthquake-resistant buildings to early warning systems and public education, Japan's comprehensive approach to disaster preparedness is a model for other nations facing similar risks. While the 1995 Kobe earthquake and the 2011 Tōhoku earthquake revealed challenges in some areas, Japan's ongoing efforts to strengthen its disaster resilience continue to be a global benchmark. With continued investment in technology, infrastructure, and public education, Japan remains at the forefront of disaster preparedness and recovery.

Appendix J: Key Terms and Concepts in Tatsuki's Prophecies

This glossary includes important terms and concepts related to Ryo Tatsuki's prophetic works, as well as broader themes in disaster preparedness and manga. It provides definitions and explanations of key concepts found in her art, along with cultural references and symbolic elements that help readers understand the depth of her work.

Key Terms Related to Prophecy and Disaster Preparedness

1. Prophecy

Definition: A prediction or vision about future events, often believed to be divinely inspired or foreseen through mystical or supernatural means. In Tatsuki's work, prophecy is often portrayed through her dreams and visions, which foresee catastrophic events like earthquakes, tsunamis, and pandemics.

Context in Tatsuki's Work: Tatsuki's prophetic storytelling taps into the human fear of the future and the inevitability of disaster. Her works ask whether the future is predestined or shaped by individual and collective action.

2. Foresight

Definition: The ability to predict or anticipate future events, often based on intuition or subconscious perception. Foresight can also refer to future-oriented thinking, focusing on preparedness and prevention.

Context in Tatsuki's Work: Tatsuki's characters often display foresight in the form of premonitory dreams, sensing disasters or crises before they happen, a theme that influences how her work deals with survival and resilience.

3. Subconscious Signals

Definition: Information perceived below the level of conscious awareness, often influencing intuitive decisions or predictions. These signals can mani-fest as feelings, dreams, or premonitions.

Context in Tatsuki's Work: Tatsuki's prophetic visions are often interpreted as subconscious signals—a form of psychic intuition—that reflect the broader psychological and emotional climate of a society in crisis.

4. Disaster Preparedness

Definition: The actions taken in advance to prepare for natural or man-made disasters, including safety measures, education, and infrastructure to reduce the impact of catastrophic events.

Context in Tatsuki's Work: The theme of disaster preparedness is woven into Tatsuki's narratives, where her characters must navigate apocalyptic scenarios with limited resources, emphasizing human adaptability and community resilience.

5. Crisis Management

Definition: The process of preparing for and managing large-scale emergency situations, including coordination of resources, information, and support to minimize damage and loss.

Context in Tatsuki's Work: Tatsuki's prophetic stories often explore how individuals and societies respond to large-scale crises, focusing on the psychological and emotional toll of managing such disasters.

Key Concepts in Tatsuki's Works

1. Apocalyptic Narrative

Definition: A genre or narrative structure in which the world faces significant destruction, often through natural disasters, war, or environmental collapse. Apocalyptic stories commonly focus on the survival and emotional journeys of characters navigating a drastically altered world.

Context in Tatsuki's Work: Tatsuki frequently explores apocalyptic scenarios, where her characters experience the aftermath of catastrophic events. These narratives delve into human resilience, survival instincts, and the psychological aftermath of disaster.

2. Psychological Resilience

Definition: The ability of individuals or groups to adapt to adversity and recover from trauma, particularly after experiencing significant loss or devastation. Resilience is a key theme in Tatsuki's prophetic works, where characters must learn to cope with the emotional fallout of foreseen catastrophes.

Context in Tatsuki's Work: In many of her stories, characters are forced to overcome the emotional and mental toll of living through predicted disasters, with a focus on their personal growth, coping mechanisms, and ability to rebuild their lives.

3. The Hero's Journey

Definition: A narrative structure where a protagonist undergoes a transformation through trials, challenges, and growth, ultimately leading to personal enlightenment or self-realization. This concept is often used in mythology, literature, and modern storytelling.

Context in Tatsuki's Work: While Tatsuki's work often focuses on collective struggles, elements of the hero's journey are present in the characters' emotional arcs, where they evolve from being passive victims of prophecy to active agents in shaping their futures.

4. Dystopia

Definition: A society or world in which the living conditions are extremely poor, often due to oppressive governments, environmental disaster, or technological failure. Dystopian settings are frequently used in speculative fiction to explore societal issues.

Context in Tatsuki's Work: Tatsuki's works often explore dystopian futures shaped by predictive visions of disaster. These narratives focus not just on the destruction of society, but also on how individuals and communities can survive and rebuild in such a world.

5. Fate vs. Free Will

Definition: The philosophical debate over whether the course of events in life is pre-determined by external forces or whether individuals have the power to make independent choices that shape their destiny.

Context in Tatsuki's Work: Tatsuki's prophetic stories often address the conflict between fate (the inevitable future) and free will (the ability to act and influence outcomes). Her characters grapple with whether they can change the future or if they are merely following a preordained path.

6. Symbolism in Art

Definition: The use of symbols or images to represent abstract ideas, emotions, or concepts. In manga and graphic novels, symbolism can enhance thematic elements and deepen the emotional impact of the story.

Context in Tatsuki's Work: Tatsuki employs symbolism in her art to reflect the psychological states of her characters and the societal impact of the disasters they face. For example, storm imagery might represent emotional turmoil or impending disaster, while broken objects may symbolize loss and the need for reconstruction.

Cultural References and Symbolic Elements in Tatsuki's Art

1. Shinto and Buddhist Influences

Shinto and Buddhism, the two primary religious traditions in Japan, often feature prominently in Tatsuki's works. Shinto emphasizes the spiritual significance of nature and the interconnectedness of all things, while Buddhism focuses on the impermanence of life and the quest for enlightenment through suffering and renewal.

Context in Tatsuki's Work: Tatsuki's prophetic visions often involve themes of rebirth, suffering, and emotional purification, which align with Buddhist teachings. Elements of nature—such as storms, floods, and earthquakes—are symbolic of transformation and change, which resonate with Shinto beliefs about the power of natural forces.

2. The "Kintsugi" Metaphor

Definition: Kintsugi is the Japanese art of repairing broken pottery with gold or silver lacquer, creating visible seams that highlight the cracks rather than hiding them. This process symbolizes the beauty of imperfection and the acceptance of past trauma.

Context in Tatsuki's Work: The concept of kintsugi is metaphorically reflected in Tatsuki's narratives, where the destruction of society and the emotional scars of her characters are acknowledged and transformed into new strengths. Her characters often rebuild their lives and relationships after catastrophic events, emphasizing the idea of finding beauty in brokenness.

3. "Mono no Aware" (The Pathos of Things)

Definition: Mono no aware is a Japanese term that refers to the awareness of the impermanence of life, coupled with a deep appreciation for the fleeting beauty of things. It evokes a sense of nostalgia and transience, acknowledging that everything, from human life to natural phenomena, is temporary.

Context in Tatsuki's Work: Tatsuki's prophetic art often conveys a sense of mono no aware, as characters navigate the emotional fallout of impending disasters. This sense of transience is central to her exploration of human fragility and resilience.

Ryo Tatsuki's prophetic works combine deeply personal and societal themes with a rich tapestry of cultural symbolism, philosophical exploration, and psychological depth. The terms and concepts outlined in this appendix reflect the intricate layers of meaning in her stories, where prophecy, human resilience, and emotional transformation are at the forefront. By understanding the key ideas and cultural references in her art, readers can gain a deeper appreciation for the emotional and symbolic depth of Tatsuki's work, as well as the universal themes that resonate with audiences worldwide.

Appendix K: Resources for Further Reading

This curated list of books, articles, scholarly papers, and other resources provides readers with an opportunity to deepen their understanding of prophecy, intuitive art, and the psychological aspects of premonitions. Additionally, it offers recommendations for exploring prophetic and apocalyptic literature, both fiction and nonfiction, as well as documentaries and films about prophetic figures and disaster preparedness.

Books on Prophecy, Intuitive Art, and Premonitions

1. "The Art of Prophecy: A Journey into the Minds of Seers" by Lorna Byrne

Overview: This book offers insights into how prophecies emerge from deep intuition and personal visions. Lorna Byrne, a well-known Irish mystic, discusses her own experiences of prophecy and how such visions have shaped her life and the lives of others.

Relevance: For readers interested in understanding the psychological and spiritual dimensions of prophetic visions, particularly those that transcend the physical realm.

2. "The Prophet" by Kahlil Gibran

Overview: A philosophical and poetic text that touches on themes of love, pain, joy, and the future. Though not a typical "prophecy" book, Gibran's work delves into universal wisdom that can feel prophetic in its timeless and spiritual insights.

Relevance: A key literary work that reflects the emotional and spiritual resonance of prophecy, exploring how personal insight can lead to universal truths.

3. "The Psychic Pathway: A Workbook for Reawakening the Voice of Your Soul" by Sophia Center

Overview: A guide to understanding and developing psychic and intuitive abilities, this book offers exercises and methods for honing one's psychic sensitivity and recognizing premonitions.

Relevance: For those interested in the psychological and intuitive aspects of prophecy and the development of clairvoyant or precognitive abilities.

4. "The Gift of Prophecy: Understanding the Gift and How to Develop It" by Jack Deere

Overview: This book explores prophetic giftings and offers practical advice on how to develop this ability. Deere provides both biblical and experiential perspectives on prophecy and its role in daily life.

Relevance: A Christian perspective on prophecy that delves into spiritual practices and the psychological impact of prophetic revelation.

Articles and Scholarly Papers on Prophecy, Intuition, and Premonitions

1. "Intuition and Decision Making: A Psychological Perspective" by Gerd Gigerenzer

Overview: This article discusses how intuition plays a significant role in human decision-making, especially in uncertain and complex situations. Gigerenzer examines the cognitive mechanisms behind intuitive decision-making and its relationship to prophetic foresight.

Relevance: Essential reading for understanding how intuition and subconscious signals may lead to premonitions or seemingly prophetic insights.

2. "Psychology of Prophecy: A Review of Cognitive and Psychological Approaches" by David E. Schmitt

Overview: This paper reviews the psychological frameworks behind the phenomenon of prophecy, focusing on cognitive and psychodynamic theories. It explores how subconscious factors contribute to the perception of future events.

Relevance: For readers interested in scientific and psychological perspectives on how prophetic visions might arise from subconscious processes.

3. "Premonition and Dream Prophecy: A Psychological Interpretation" by Stanley Krippner

Overview: Krippner discusses the role of dreams and premonitions in human psychology, exploring how the subconscious mind processes information and sometimes "foresees" future events.

Relevance: A key paper for understanding the psychological origins of premonitions and their role in art and prophecy.

Prophetic and Apocalyptic Literature (Fiction and Nonfiction)

1. "The Road" by Cormac McCarthy

Overview: A dystopian novel that portrays a father and son's journey through a post-apocalyptic landscape. McCarthy's prose offers a stark and emotionally complex narrative about survival, resilience, and the human will to live in the face of catastrophe.

Relevance: This novel is a literary exploration of the aftermath of apocalyptic events, focusing on the emotional and psychological toll of living in a predicted future.

2. "The Left Behind Series" by Tim LaHaye and Jerry B. Jenkins

Overview: A series of Christian apocalyptic novels that portray the events leading up to and following the Second Coming of Christ. The series follows a group of people left behind after the rapture, dealing with the implications of prophecy in a biblical context.

Relevance: A cultural phenomenon within Christian prophecy literature, the series discusses themes of end times, fate, and personal transformation in the face of a prophesied future.

3. "The Coming Plague: Newly Emerging Diseases in a World Out of Balance" by Laurie Garrett

Overview: This nonfiction book explores the history and future of pandemics, focusing on how diseases have emerged, spread, and shaped human history. Garrett discusses the role of prophecy in predicting pandemics and other global health threats.

Relevance: An insightful nonfiction work that examines how scientific foresight and prophetic predictions have intersected in the realm of public health crises.

4. "The Last Policeman" by Ben H. Winters

Overview: A detective novel set in a world on the brink of extinction, where an asteroid is predicted to destroy Earth in six months. The protagonist, a police officer, continues solving crimes despite the imminent end of the world.

Relevance: An exploration of how humanity reacts to foreseen catastrophe, fate, and the moral dilemmas of living in the shadow of an impending disaster.

Documentaries and Films on Prophetic Figures and Disaster Preparedness

1. "Prophecy: The History of Prediction" (Documentary)

Overview: This documentary explores the history of prophecy and how various cultures have used visions, dreams, and psychic abilities to predict the future. It includes insights into the works of Nostradamus, Baba Vanga, and others.

Relevance: For readers interested in historical and cultural perspectives on prophecy, offering an overview of significant prophetic figures and how their predictions have been interpreted over time.

2. "Inside Fukushima: The Nuclear Disaster" (Documentary)

Overview: This documentary examines the 2011 Fukushima Daiichi Nuclear Power Plant disaster, caused by the Tōhoku earthquake and tsunami, and provides a detailed look at how Japan responded to the nuclear crisis and what lessons were learned for disaster preparedness.

Relevance: A real-world exploration of how predicted events—like natural disasters—trigger long-lasting societal and environmental impacts.

3. "The Day After Tomorrow" (Film, 2004)

Overview: A disaster film that portrays the catastrophic effects of climate change, as a series of extreme weather events leads to the collapse of global civilization. The film explores themes of fate, human response to disaster, and survival in the face of overwhelming odds.

Relevance: A fictionalized interpretation of apocalyptic predictions, with a focus on climate crisis and how humanity might react to a future shaped by predictive warnings.

4. "An Inconvenient Truth" (Documentary, 2006)

Overview: This documentary, featuring former U.S. Vice President Al Gore, addresses the urgency of climate change, using scientific data to predict the potential disastrous effects of global warming.

Relevance: A real-world example of predictive science and how prophetic warnings about climate change are influencing public policy and global consciousness.

This resource list offers a diverse set of materials for those interested in exploring the concept of prophecy and its cultural, psychological, and artistic impact. By diving into the works of Ryo Tatsuki, alongside related literature, academic studies, and media, readers can further understand how prophecy— whether seen through the lens of intuitive art, science, or culture—shapes our understanding of the future, the consequences of human actions, and the resilience of the human spirit in the face of uncertainty.

Made in the USA
Monee, IL
07 July 2025

20677114R00066